Praise for *The Plugged-In Manager*

"*The Plugged-In Manager* succinctly addresses the people, process, and organizational issues often overlooked in the rush to adopt emerging technologies like social media. A must-read, it helps you harness the power of collaborative technologies for more successful business, customer, and partner interactions."
—Laura Ramos, vice president, industry marketing, Xerox Document Outsourcing Services US; and B2B marketing blogger

"This book is a great reference for innovation managers in companies of all sizes. Through numerous case studies, Terri Griffith shows how mixing technology, processes, and people can create a sustainable environment for growth and innovation."
—Ben Shahshahani, vice president, Yahoo! Labs

"*The Plugged-In Manager* is the result of Terri Griffith's twenty-five-year love for, and deep experience with, technology and organizations. Her experience and commitment—coupled with insights that come from steel companies to sport venues—produce clear guidance for everyone, whether working on their own or inside a big firm."
—Andrew Hargadon, professor and founding director, UC Davis Center for Entrepreneurship; and author, *How Breakthroughs Happen: The Surprising Truth About How Companies Innovate*

"This book is an up-to-the-minute guide to the evolving fundamentals of management in our tech-savvy and largely web-based lifestyles. Instead of ignoring the impact of information technology on managing teams, Terri helps her readers leverage it and become more impactful—and relevant—business leaders."
—Mark Weiner, senior vice president, worldwide marketing, Virtela; and faculty, Santa Clara University

THE
PLUGGED-IN
MANAGER

THE
PLUGGED-IN
MANAGER

GET IN TUNE WITH
YOUR PEOPLE, TECHNOLOGY,
AND ORGANIZATION TO THRIVE

TERRI L. GRIFFITH

Foreword by John Hagel III

JOSSEY-BASS
A Wiley Imprint
www.josseybass.com

Published by Jossey-Bass
A Wiley Imprint
989 Market Street, San Francisco, CA 94103-1741—www.josseybass.com

Jossey-Bass books and products are available through most bookstores. To contact Jossey-Bass directly
call our Customer Care Department within the U.S. at 800-956-7739, outside the U.S. at 317-572-
3986, or fax 317-572-4002.

Jossey-Bass also publishes its books in a variety of electronic formats. Some content that appears in
print may not be available in electronic books.

Library of Congress Cataloging-in-Publication Data
Griffith, Terri.
  The plugged-in manager : get in tune with your people, technology, and organization to thrive /
Terri L. Griffith. — 1st ed.
      p. cm.
  Includes bibliographical references and index.
  ISBN 978-0-470-90355-1 (cloth); ISBN 978-1-118-11254-0 (ebk); 978-1-118-11255-7 (ebk); 978-1-118-
11256-4 (ebk)
    1. Organizational effectiveness.   2. Management—Social aspects.   3. Information technology—
Management.   4. Technological innovations—Management.   I. Title.
  HD58.9.G755 2012
  658—dc23
                                    2011029318

Printed in the United States of America
FIRST EDITION
HB Printing   10 9 8 7 6 5 4 3 2 1

CONTENTS

FOREWORD

Terri Griffith has written an important and timely book. We live in increasingly challenging times, in which performance pressure mounts irresistibly and continually, without any end in sight. The disruptions that play out with increasing frequency and severity around us call into question our most basic assumptions about what is required for business and personal success.

In this kind of environment, there is a natural and understandable desire for quick and simple answers that can relieve the pressure and stress and give us a sense of security. Terri resists this pressure. A key message in her book is that there are no silver bullets to help us, even though we may desperately want to believe that there are. Perhaps even more bravely, she asserts that there are not even recipes—simple and consistent instructions with ingredients in precise proportions that can be followed in all situations.

The complex systems we live and work in do not afford us the simplicity of recipes designed to apply the same formula in all contexts. To make progress, we must first understand that context matters and that the approaches we take need to be tailored and adapted to the specific context. This leads to an emphasis on a key practice for plugged-in managers: They must be prepared to stop, look, and listen, developing a deep awareness of context.

There is another message that Terri consistently emphasizes throughout the book. Even once we have developed a deep awareness of our current context and engaged in the hard work required to develop an approach tailored to that context, our work as plugged-in managers has just begun. In an increasingly fluid world, context evolves rapidly. That means not only that our management approaches must be tailored to our context, but also that our approaches need to flexibly and continually adapt to our changing context. This leads to Terri's emphasis on listening—constantly observing how our management approaches are performing, and learning from that experience to evolve our approaches in ways that drive sustained performance improvement. We live in a dynamic world, and our approach to that world needs to become equally dynamic.

To put it in my own words, we are moving from a world of stocks to one of flows. In the past, business success hinged on acquiring a powerful set of proprietary knowledge stocks, aggressively protecting those knowledge stocks, and then as efficiently as possible extracting the value from those knowledge stocks and delivering it to the marketplace. This was the world of precisely and tightly specified (and standardized) business processes that sought to remove friction and maximize efficiency. Although those business processes might occasionally need to be reconfigured in infrequent gales of business process redesign, the key goal was to enhance predictability and eliminate exceptions.

But with the accelerating pace of change, we face a fundamental challenge. Whatever knowledge stocks we may have, they are depreciating at an accelerating rate. In this environment, business success increasingly depends on our ability to participate effectively in a broader range of knowledge flows so that we can refresh our knowledge stocks more rapidly. The plugged-in manager is one who learns to harness knowledge flows in ways that create growing economic value over time, rather than clinging to existing knowledge stocks and squeezing them ever more vigorously in a vain effort to extract the next increment of value.

This is a fundamental shift, something that I call "the big shift" that challenges our most basic assumptions about business and work. Companies unable to navigate this shift will fall by the wayside, while others, including companies not yet formed today, will master the new practices required to succeed in a more challenging environment and create enormous wealth in the process.

For those companies, Terri's book will be an essential navigation guide. *The Plugged-In Manager* does not offer a precise course to follow, but it does offer essential insight regarding the ingredients required for business success.

Terri appropriately emphasizes the need to blend together three elements—people, technology, and organizational processes —as we design our management approaches. None of these on its own will provide us with the answers we need. Nor can we focus on each element in isolation. These elements work together as a complex and evolving system. The real power comes from integrating and blending these three elements so that each element works to reinforce and amplify the power of the other elements.

In a world increasingly entranced with technology, this is a powerful antidote to the claims of technology evangelists who attribute miraculous powers to their favorite new technologies. The truth that Terri's book drives home is that technology in isolation is useless and perhaps even dangerous. Only by integrating technology effectively into a specific social and business context can we release its latent power. By staying focused on the people and organizational processes that must be supported by the technology, we can develop a more realistic appreciation of its possibilities. In doing this, we can avoid becoming carried away by the latest technology fad and stay focused on the real capability of the technology. As Terri points out, often the answer may be to forgo a new technology altogether and focus instead on how to more effectively deploy existing technology to support the people and processes of the firm.

The real power of Terri's book, however, is that she goes beyond a discussion of the three elements required to develop an integrated and effective management approach. Her real focus is on three management practices that the plugged-in manager must develop in order to effectively integrate new systems. The three elements—which are *stop-look-listen, mixing,* and *sharing*—constitute a powerful way to develop a more dynamic approach to management and guard against the constant threat of complacency; that is, of believing that one has finally come up with a system that will have no further need of change.

The feedback loop of stop-look-listen, with its emphasis on the importance of experimentation and after action reviews, is particularly important to thriving in our dynamic world. Deep awareness of one's context and how it is continually changing, combined with constant reassessment of business initiatives, is essential to coping with accelerating change.

As Terri points out, it is the integration of these three practices that contains the real power. On the one hand, these approaches enhance a vision of possibilities, revealing new horizons that may not even have been visible before. On the other hand, these approaches help to develop a wisdom about capabilities and limitations that helps guide managers along pragmatic pathways to nurture potential and possibilities.

Managers can pursue these plugged-in practices at any level in an organization. But the real opportunity is to harness layered approaches to plugged-in management, wherein each level of an organization amplifies and reinforces the plugged-in management approaches pursued in other layers. Rather than becoming an obstacle to such initiatives, the organization becomes a platform to stimulate and reward such initiatives at all levels.

Terri is appropriately skeptical about the role of training in developing plugged-in managers. Although some basic frameworks and examples are important to bring these practices to life, there is no substitute for actual engagement in the practices. As soon as you finish this book, the best thing you can do is to find some context in which you can begin to apply these practices and tailor your approach to your specific needs. Learning by doing and working with others is the only way that these practices will come alive and their true value become apparent.

John Hagel III
Coauthor, *The Power of Pull*

To my parents, Kay and Neil Griffith, lifelong teachers.

THE
PLUGGED-IN
MANAGER

chapter
ONE

Plugging In to the Twenty-First Century

Imagine this: You are an executive at an online retailing company. A mid-level customer service representative at your company has begun tracking and responding to customer comments on Facebook and Twitter without clearing his actions with management. The response from customers has been great, and you've even gotten some popular press coverage. But this isn't a sanctioned activity. What will you do?

1. Contact the service rep and ask him to stop until you've had a chance to clear this approach with company security and marketing.
2. Contact the service rep and congratulate him on the great idea. Let other executives know about the service representative's success.

1

3. Add a computer monitoring tool to keep track of the customer and service rep activities on these public sites. Get involved only if you see a problem building.
4. Write a new company policy about employee actions on social media sites.
5. Organize and train a team of customer service reps to help the first service rep as public interest grows. Have this team suggest guidelines and tools for other areas of the organization to use.
6. Automatically block access to social networking sites from company computers.

In our ongoing research, my colleagues and I are finding that people's answers are very different depending on how "plugged in" they are. I call "plugged-in" managers those who are able to see choices across each of an organization's dimensions of people, technology, and organizational processes and then to mix them together into new and powerful organizational strategies, structures, and practices.

What set the plugged-in managers apart in their responses to this scenario was their apparent comfort with letting the use of the technology and the organizational policies and procedures emerge.[1] Plugged-in managers were more likely to write a new company policy about employee actions on social media sites and to organize and train a separate team of customer service reps to help the first service rep as public interest grows than the less plugged-in respondents were, and the plugged-in managers were far less likely to add a computer monitoring tool or block access to social media sites. The plugged-in managers were focused on working with their people to develop tools and rules that could evolve with the situation. Less plugged-in respondents seemed to want to control the situation.

None of the respondents had a clear-cut framework to help them make their decisions. With this book I hope to change that.

Why Plug In Now?

Social networking is not the only organizational challenge confronting organizations today. We live and work in a world that is constantly changing in terms of the ways we communicate, collaborate, make decisions, find jobs, and entertain ourselves. Our computers shift with increasing speed through software revisions and the introduction of smaller, yet often more powerful, hardware. Every day we see some expansion in the vast variety of how and where we can connect to the Internet and what we find when we get there. Tools that used to be just tools are now "smart" and may do their own connecting to the Internet or store their information for later use. (I'm thinking about how my cell phone is linked to my running shoes via a pedometer app, which in turn links to a social networking website to help me keep track of my activity levels.)

Your organization most likely needs to operate globally, work jointly with other organizations to take on big tasks, and share research and results with employees, customers, clients, and partners as never before. The people inside your organization are probably more diverse in terms of age, technological sophistication, and cultural background than just a few years ago. You and your colleagues can generally expect to have multiple careers.

To be effective in this changing world, you need to understand how to work and manage in a way that brings together all of the related organizational processes, technology tools, and people populating our workplaces. Although I'd like to simplify and call these three elements the building blocks of organizations, I can't. None of the three can stand alone. The processes, technology, and people (with their knowledge, skills, and abilities) must all be considered and dealt with together, not as independent or isolated factors, for our work and organizations to be effective.

In other words, you need to plug in to effectively work and manage in the twenty-first century.

Plugging in means having the ability to mix together these three elements:

- The knowledge, skills, and abilities of the people you are working with
- The technology tools of work (everything from email to the size and type of tools a crew would use to build a fence)
- The way you organize your work (for example, teams spread all over the world, the size of the fence-building crew, formal and informal leadership, hiring and pay plans)

You typically can't just make a change to one of those three dimensions without making an adjustment to the others as well.

Think about it this way: Let's say your organization wants you to team up with a group in another country and time zone. You may need to change your work hours. You must be sure the team has access to a good teleconferencing technology and gets some basic training on how to use that technology. You can't just declare that everyone should start working together and neglect "mixing" in some other changes to support it. You have to be thinking about all your technology tools, organizational processes, and people as you determine how to get work done with the other group.

Keep in mind, too, that there's probably no single best way to get the work done. Some teams use the latest and greatest technologies (and make sure they have the latest and greatest skills to use them), while other teams decide to stick to phone calls and faxing notes around. You just need to be sure that the approach works well as a whole system.

Getting plugged in does not require that you have x-ray vision into human capabilities, or be an expert with the raw materials of technology tools, or know the intricacies of organizational operations. You can work with other people who do have deep expertise in the specific area. You just need to be aware of your options and realize that designing work as a system, rather than just changing one thing at a time, is essential to organizational success.[2]

Plugged-in management is important no matter what your organizational setting, whether you are in a high-tech software company, heavy manufacturing, or a health non-profit. Even a crew building a fence will be better off if they balance the technologies they have access to with the size and skills of the team members. A bigger gas-powered posthole digger may mean the work goes faster, but you need two heavy people to run it, and those people may need to take more breaks. A good team leader, or a strong self-managing team, will have taken a look at the project and brought the right tools and people for the job. They also will have made thoughtful choices about how to manage quality, speed, and safety. Different projects may use different pay plans; for example, pay by the quality of the project, pay by experience or skill, and or a bonus for finishing early with no injuries.

Again, there is no one best way, but all the parts have to be taken into account and mixed together purposefully.

In other words, organizational success more likely occurs when all three critical dimensions—technology, organization, and human capabilities and motivations—are taken into account concurrently. There are no silver bullets. Even excellent management actions, if restricted to a single dimension, can never have the same success as when all three dimensions are managed together. Fredrick Brooks, summarizing the issues in a classic 1986 article, notes "There is no single development, in either technology or in management technique, that by itself promises even one order of magnitude improvement in productivity, in reliability, in simplicity."[3]

Plugged-In Management for All

Everyone in your organization needs to get more plugged in. Individual contributors use their plugged-in expertise to decide the best way to do their work. Members of work teams use plugged-in skills to help the team find the best combinations of people, tools, and organizational processes for a particular task. Managers use plugged-in approaches to build organizations that are effective and efficient. Organizational leaders use plugged-in abilities to create a vision for the future.

Plugged-in management applies to all organizational tasks and settings: from recruiting to sales presentations, from managing virtual teams to building streamlined innovation systems, from decisions about the latest management fad to coal mining—an industry for which some of these ideas were first considered in the 1950s.[4] People, technology, and policies and procedures are foundational to our organizational actions. Success in management—and in business in general—demands the simultaneous, interwoven consideration of these foundational components:

○ **People:** How many there are, the skills they have, the basics of human reactions (people go toward rewards and away from punishment), their demographic backgrounds, the languages they speak, and so on.

○ **Technology:** Software applications, network infrastructures, and even hard technologies like assembly lines and toilets (for example, in hospital rooms); the quality, access, integration, and support of these technology systems.

○ **Organizational Policies, Procedures, and Processes:** Approaches to recruiting, hiring (both contract and permanent), training, evaluation, pay, and other performance management activities; team or individual contributor-focused structures; layers of management; focus on outsourcing; and the like. For simplicity, I'll label this component Organizational Process.

Our work is not done in silos, yet much of our technology and work infrastructures are built as if it were. Management isn't just about organizational process. Management isn't just about technology. Management certainly isn't just about people. Too often, discussions of management look at people, technology, *or* organization. Rarely do we see the three addressed in an integrated, whole-system way. When we do, the result is game-changing.

What's Ahead

Plugged-in management skill is one of the most important capabilities a modern manager can have. Having a clear strategic vision, "emotional intelligence," and other soft skills is key, but the big impact comes from knowing how to work with people, technology, and organizational process all at the same time to reach that strategic vision. In this book, you will discover the reality of the modern business landscape and learn how to mix people, technology, and organization into strong, flexible business solutions.

This chapter and the next introduce the concept of plugged-in management and set us on our journey. This first chapter outlines the critical need for plugged-in management and summarizes its broad benefits to managers and organizations today. It provides a road map for the rest of the book. Chapter Two defines the landscape in terms of the many different ways that modern organizations are becoming increasingly complex in terms of the people, technology, and organizational process within them.

Part One: The Three Practices of Plugged-In Managers

The heart of the book is organized around three practices that plugged-in managers consistently demonstrate:

1. Plugged-in managers assess the situation and scan the environment for resources and pitfalls. They "Stop-Look-Listen" in the same way we all do before crossing a busy street or starting to cook a meal for family or friends. They *stop* to reflect on the situation:

- Is this an incremental change in your organization or a major strategic move?
- Is this a weeknight quick dinner or a holiday repast?
- Do you have to go to the store, or are you ready to begin chopping?

They *look* at available data (or collect some via simple experiments) to narrow down the possibilities:

- What do you already know that will help you with this project?
- What recipes have you tried and how did they work?

They *listen* to feedback from others involved at the core and in connecting roles:

- What did participants in your last event say on the social networks?
- Are you seeing reductions in downtime after restructuring your call center?
- Did your guests want seconds and then ask you to share your recipes?

2. Plugged-in managers *mix* together solutions that balance the people, technology, and organizational process involved. They know that there are many ways to make a great meal, but all involve appropriately blending and balancing available ingredients and dishes.

3. Plugged-in managers *share* their savvy and skills with others. They publicly model good plugged-in management and give their colleagues the chance to build their own plugging-in skills through experience. Richer outcomes (and meals) happen when more people are involved. If you design work or a meal just for one, you are limited in what you can do. Plugged-in managers know that the more they share and integrate their choices with others, the stronger the outcome. The ideas and flavors will be more integrated, and the cooking process will become more aligned over time as everyone learns how their contributions best fit in the mix.

Chapters Three, Four, and Five focus on these three practices, respectively. They include deep examples from Providence Regional Medical Center, Southwest Airlines, and Nucor as context for understanding plugged-in management in action. (I owe a great debt to the many CEOs, managers, and individual contributors who have allowed me to include their stories as illustrations of these practices and their success.) I also lay out strategies for building on your plugged-in management skills. We all have some plugged-in management expertise, and even people with significant skills and experience can continue to learn to be more efficient and to fine-tune their approach.

Part Two: Learning to Plug In

Part Two is about developing your own skills for plugging in. Chapter Six is a chance for you to evaluate your own plugged-in management approach across a variety of examples. I've included two short assessment tools that will help you compare your own approach to those of some of the people mentioned in the book. The results may surprise you. You may even want to try the tools now, before digging into the background and examples in Parts One and Two. You may also want to ask your teammates at some point to assess their own base levels of plugged-in management skills.

To round out your action plan for honing your skills, Chapter Seven offers opportunities to learn how to develop and apply plugged-in management in a series of complex situations. Chapter Eight then closes with an example of a layered approach to plugged-in management, in which the true power of plugging in comes together: You have plugged-in skills, your colleagues do as well, and your organization is built in a way that supports and develops plugged-in action.

The twenty-first century presents us with both challenges and opportunities. In the next chapter, I will point to specific reasons for getting more plugged in and illustrate some of the ways different organizations are thriving by putting plugged-in management to work.

chapter TWO

Why You Need Plugged-In Management

Modern organizations are increasingly complex across three critical dimensions: people who interact within and with our organizations, technology tools, and organizational processes. Finding ways to effectively mix these dimensions together is the goal of plugged-in management, yet the raw materials you start with become more complex every day. In addition to the complexity of the underlying dimensions, you also have to deal with systemic shifts that are enabled by these changing technologies, organizational realities, and people. For example, there is increased transparency, both across and within organizations. Expectations are blurring what was once a sharply defined who knows what and who does what. Whether roles and relationships are blurred or not, you still need to manage them in order to be effective. There are great opportunities if you practice plugged-in management—and great risks if you do not.

Changing Technology, Organizations, and People

Technology tools are critical to how you get work done. In some cases the technology may act like—or be!—the plumbing. Regular plumbing certainly isn't simple, but at least it's been around a long while—and it can be seen and touched (if you don't mind crawling around under your house). You also have information "plumbing" to deal with, and its complexity is multiplied by the fact that few of us are expert enough to see how it really works, even if we are willing to crawl under the house . . . or behind the desk . . . or search through our manuals. Most of us don't know exactly how our telephone works, but in today's world we need a bit of that knowledge to be effective in even day-to-day tasks. Most of us at least know that if our cell phone isn't connecting we should move to a window, but so much else that could help us remains unknown.

Modern technology tools also change more often than plumbing does. Sometimes the change is for the better, but the change is still something to be evaluated and understood. In the case of information technology tools (the Internet, our company's private network, our own personal social networks, how we pay our vendors), the rate of information we have access to is growing at an almost unimaginable rate. At Google's Atmosphere 2010 conference, Google CEO Eric Schmidt invited four hundred chief information officers to think of the amount of information created between the birth of the world and 2003. He claims that we now create that same amount of information every two days.[1]

Organizations are also more complex than those of the past. Organizations are global, partnered with other organizations, and often involve teams of people who have never met face to face. Although this was certainly true in decades past, the variety and fluidity of how people do work in organizations continues to grow. The networks within and across organizations are both more complicated and, like technologies, sometimes hard to see.

The people within today's organizations also add to the complexity you must manage. Your employees, partners, and customers are more diverse due to globalization and the crossing of generations with vastly different backgrounds.

Why We Must Plug In Now

In the following sections, I highlight examples of how technology, organizations, and people are changing in important ways—and how plugging in can help you thrive in this environment. Even though I show the examples of technology, organization, and people separately, keep in mind that the tensions and solutions come from managing them together.

We Must Keep Up with Technology

Plugging in now is imperative, in the face of technology that is incredibly complex, increasingly abstract, and constantly changing.

Consider how organizations decide to keep their computing local or to move some or all of their efforts into the "cloud." Google, Amazon, Salesforce.com, and many others are looking to a world where the Internet is your computer: Your work exists in a cloud of computer resources managed by someone else. The box on your desk with a keyboard can just be the tool you use to access your data and applications. For example, I am writing this chapter in the cloud via Google Docs (Google's word processing application). If you read your email on the Web via Yahoo! Mail, Gmail, or other web email services, your email is already in the cloud.

As its name suggests, cloud computing is a technology that you can't physically touch. Not even the major application and portal providers can agree on a definition or a best use. What should be in the cloud? All or some of your data? All or some of your applications? You may not know where your information is being physically stored, so if there's an earthquake in California or a flood in Missouri, should you be concerned? You have to read carefully to understand the rights you have regarding your data and whether and how it is being backed up. Given that access is via the Internet, there may be times the information isn't accessible. The provider of your cloud probably offers different levels of service and then lets you pick what you are willing to pay for. How do you decide? How do you know which aspects of your business are appropriate for cloud computing and which aspects should stay under your physical control? *BusinessWeek* issued a special report in August 2008 describing their view of how cloud computing is changing the world.[2] But over three years later, the answers to these questions are still not clear.

Plugged-in management gives you an outline of how to address these questions. Awareness of the roles of technology, organizational process, and people involved gives you a start. As a technology, cloud computing is spreading, dropping in cost, and expanding in the number of available applications. These technology dynamics motivate us to make an assessment of whether or not the technology can benefit our company or individual work practice.

Knowing that there are also organizational and people implications to consider gives us a starting point. From the organizational perspective, you need to understand the cross-organizational relationships that are at the heart of cloud computing: You are outsourcing the storage of your information and computer applications.

Your people are also part of your consideration. Our problem-solving ability and decisions are based on our "mental models" of how the system works. As long as these mental models are moderately accurate, you can make decent decisions about how to use technology tools. Your employees probably understand how to manage the information on their own laptop, but do they have an accurate model of how to manage their information in the cloud?

You may need to put together new training to help them with this transition. Accurate models of cloud computing will include a knowledge of where the data is stored (for example, on your local PC, inside the corporate firewall, on a commercial secure server); how often the data is backed up; whether syncing between the local PC and the cloud version is automatic; where the application is running (for example, whether you will be able to use the application when on a plane or at a vendor's site where you may or may not have Internet access); whether you will need to worry about updates to the software (perhaps not, if the application is on the cloud); and much more.

The difficulty with abstract concepts such as cloud computing and electronic books is that they don't give us much on which to base our sense making. Ancient technologies had a concreteness that helped us grasp their use and functioning. I'm watching the light on my backup hard drive flicker and am comforted by the fact that it is backing up my laptop. Just now the Save icon flashed on my screen, suggesting that Google is saving this document. Which one is more real? The light or the icon? My own drive or the vast data storage systems owned by Google?

The more abstract the technology, the more implementation needs to focus on helping users develop their mental models. However, this may mean increased implementation time and budget. Not paying this price will likely result in users making uninformed decisions about how they manage their computing environment—an expensive outcome if that data is lost or compromised. Practicing plugged-in management by taking the technology, organizational, and people dimensions into account when making adoption and implementation decisions means you are more likely to make effective decisions concerning flexible, complicated technologies.

Our Organizations Have Been Transformed

Today, our organizations are global, they are partnered with other organizations, and they often involve teams of people who have never met face to face. Wim Elfrink, the chief globalization officer of Cisco, said in 2007, "We are at the edge of a market transition . . . globalization is in effect about our ability to connect the dots, uniting the right people at the right moment at the right place at the right time."[3]

Having the right people at the right time . . . Organizations are all about having the right people at the right time to work on the right projects with the right tools. The issue today is that there is greater access to a greater percentage of the right people. We are less constrained by location or organizational membership, given both our ability to collaborate via the Internet and organizations' new openness to both formal and informal alliances—that is, if we can keep a handle on the increased complexity. Plugged-in management can help with that.

Electronic communication and commerce provide access to new markets and can reduce the cost of doing business for many organizations. This is a powerful transition in all industries, but even more so in cases where the work itself has a strong electronic component. Many modern jobs include work processes and products that are amenable to electronic presentation and/or transportation. The point is that modern technology has enabled a thinning of physical organizational boundaries.

Who you work for and who works for your company is less clear than in the past. You or your coworkers may find your work through services like Elance.com—kind of an eBay for project work. Your customers may provide you with your next product direction through a website set up like MyStarbucks.com. You may help Facebook translate its pages into your native language, just for fun. Who's working for whom is less clear in today's world.

More formally, Rita Zeidner has noted that the U.S. Bureau of Labor Statistics estimates that the employment services industry will grow at twice the growth rate of the rest of the U.S. economy for the same period.[4] (The employment services industry includes organizations that help other organizations by sourcing contract employees, recruiting, or providing other human resource services.) She also mentions that human resource professionals will become more talent brokers than talent managers.

These new "employment" relationships bring with them the need for new thinking around technology tools, organizational practice, and an understanding of people. Charlene Li, founder of the Altimeter Group and past vice president at Forrester Research, writes in *Open Leadership*:

> . . . new technologies allow us to let go of control and still be in command, because better, cheaper communication tools give us the ability to be intimately familiar with what is happening with both customers and employees. The result of these new relationships is open leadership, which I define as: having the confidence and humility to give up the need to be in control while inspiring commitment from people to accomplish goals.[5]

Think carefully about how you will use these cheaper communication tools, among other technologies, to build organizations that make sense (and money), in a way that acknowledges employee skills and motivations. Plugged-in management can help with the open questions in this new environment. Plugged-in management allows you to explicitly consider the organizational form, support, and constraints around how you do your work, not just the technology and/or the social implications of working flexibly.

You need to be plugged in to handle even deeper organizational questions. The contracting and customer interactions just noted are relatively straightforward. Yes, organizations are global, partnered with other organizations, and in many cases run via virtual teams with limited physical interaction—but those are the organizations that still look the way I expect an organization to look. There are other organizations that are further out on the fringe in terms of their organizational design, in that their work is done by freelancers so indirectly connected to the organization that it's hard describe them in organizational terms. For example, a 2009 article in *Wired* magazine, "The Answer Factory," describes one organization where explicit decisions have been made to freelance some work and to turn other work over to computer algorithms.[6] Where do you put algorithms on the organizational chart? Practicing plugged-in management gives you a structure for considering the possibilities for modern organizational relationships.

Consider Google's relationship between Internet content creators and Google's use of content creators' labor. Every time that a person creates a web link (for example, in my blog I will often link to other websites as a way of providing a reference), they are adding to the intelligence Google's search engine uses to pick what search results to show.[7] If, for example, many bloggers link to a place to buy Jonathan Zittrain's book *The Future of the Internet*, then that link is likely to show up near the top of the results page for searches on Zittrain's name, the book title, applicable keywords, and so on.[8] Essentially, we've done some of Google's work for them.

The Internet enables a whole slew of new ways to create employment relationships—sometimes without people even knowing that they are working for your organization! With such flexibility and permeability in organizational boundaries, how can you think strategically about your options? Plugged-in management can be the answer. The ability to highlight your choices across technology, organizational form and practice, and people's inclinations is the first step; the ability to creatively blend them into effective strategies and tactics is the second. With the proliferation of organizations as odd as these—whether your own, a client's or customer's, or a vendor's—you need to be plugged in. Plugged-in management allows you to see how these companies work—and how they might work better.

The Organization's People Are More Diverse

Given globalization and the intermingling of generations of vastly different backgrounds, the people you work with are more diverse now than ever before. The economy is global and draws from talent pools around the world. You have a demographic bubble whereby older workers are staying in the workforce longer, given economic realities and better health, leading to greater age diversity in the workplace. This diversity can be valuable, if managed. If not managed, differences in context and skill sets can limit the effectiveness of the organization. These "people" issues are an important component of plugging in.

I recently spent time with some of the directors of SAP, IBM, NetApp, and Microsoft. They had come together to share ideas about distributed software development—a truly global endeavor. SAP, for example, has software development hubs in Germany, the United States, Israel, and India, and development facilities in many more locations. IBM topped the others in the sheer number of its facilities: twenty-two thousand software developers in sixty-one locations.[9] Although some of these organizations began their global practices for marketing reasons (to be able to more effectively respond to local market needs and conditions), they now all focus on global work and management for finding the best talent. These executives don't focus on the technology tools when they talk about the most critical management issues they face in their global businesses. Instead, they focus on being "intentional" in how they think about such issues as these:

• When to pay for travel so that team members can meet (for example, when misunderstandings happen at key design stages)

- The symbolic outcomes when executives travel to meet with teams
- The assignment of particular tasks across locations so that centers of excellence develop around certain skills—and so that development of the workforce takes place in a way that maintains motivation and value to the company

These issues focus on the people dimensions of plugged-in management. These directors work very hard to support the human component of their diverse workforce. When managers pay for team members to travel, they are being intentional about managing understanding about the work or the capabilities of the team members. They know that context is often key to this understanding and sometimes can best be supported by face-to-face interaction. When executives take the time to travel to distant sites, they are being intentional about signaling that all groups are important to the work and thus are worthy of the time and effort. When work is divided up to build experience and share interesting projects, not just save money, executives are being intentional about long-term engagement rather than short-term payoffs.

Although these particular actions each take the form of an organizational practice, the trigger comes from human conflict or concerns.

Conflict or concerns can also come from the diverse values and skills brought to work by the varied generations in the workforce today. Generations have always mingled in the workforce, but today is a uniquely complicated period. Older workers are staying on the job longer and are meeting up with a unique set of new employees who grew up in a digital world. These new employees—known as Millennials, Gen Y, or the Net Generation—were born between 1977 and 1997, and were the "first generation to be bathed in bits."[10] John Palfrey and Urs Gasser also talk about the unique nature of the newest members of the workforce. They describe as "digital natives" those born after 1980, when the first of the "social digital technologies"—the electronic bulletin boards like Usenet—came online.[11] They don't say that *everyone* born after 1980 is a digital native; rather, they apply the term to those who have always had access to networked digital technologies and know how to use them. They note that this group's life is mediated by digital technologies and that they've known nothing else. Those of us who learned to use digital technologies later in life are described as "digital immigrants."

Both the popular press and academic outlets describe how Gen Y is different from preceding generations in attitude (for example, more positive self-views, greater expectations for feedback) and capabilities (mainly, that they've grown up digital).[12] Rather than forming an obstacle, the differences can provide value in firms whose managers understand the differences across people and use the differences to trigger organizational updates and to harness the Gen Y energy and digital connections. Plugged-in management provides a way to plan for generational change and generational integration. Plugging in affirms the value of experience while providing insights into new organizational forms.

Technology tools, organizational processes, and people are relatively specific dimensions. Systemic, more abstract environmental changes also play a role in our increasing need to plug in. I'll focus on these systemic changes in the second half of this chapter.

Systemic Changes Demand Plugged-In Management

High-level systems changes—like the vast spread of social media and the downstream implications for how people get work done, the increasing transparency of organizational governance, and a blurring of organizational relationships and roles—also create a push for plugged-in management. I frequently tell my students that this is the most exciting time in the last fifty years for orga-nizational design and management. Whether an opportunity is likely to impact the whole organization or is one you can manage on your own, it takes plugging in to be able to judge these oppor-tunities and find ways to make them work effectively together.

Shifting from Push to Pull

Leading my list of systemic changes is what John Hagel, John Seely Brown, and Lang Davison describe as a transition from "push" to "pull."[13] Before the recent transformations, the pattern of how technology tools, organizational processes, and people were to be mixed together was generally pushed down from above or dic-tated from an organization to its constituents, and not always effectively. Things have changed. In the current environment there is the opportunity (and the need) to "pull" rather than waiting for opportunities to be pushed down from above. You pull by gaining access to people and resources in ways you never could before, attracting people and resources through your own partici-pation and personal and project branding, and then using these resources to contribute by achieving new outcomes from your own potential. Companies don't develop new products in a vacuum; they have "labs" where customers play an active role. Individuals don't tackle projects without support from their net-works; they reach out via social networking to see who can give them a head start. Organizations don't assume that all work is created within a functional silo; they expect that employees will reach across the organization to find the resources they need.

How you and your employees do this reaching and commu-nicating is where the value of plugged-in management appears. How do you decide what pieces of the technology infrastructure to use to access and work with your networks and other resources? Plugging in can help you mix the available people, technology tools, and organizational processes together in a way that allows you to pull support from others and be a good community member by repaying in kind, while still steering clear of the information overload that is a real risk in a pull-focused environment.

Shifting from Need-to-Know to Need-to-Share

Facebook asks us, "What's on your mind?" Twitter wonders, "What's happening?" These are social networking sites, and of course they have that focus. How about the Fortune 100? Walmart (2010 Fortune #1) has an entire webpage devoted to all the ways you can stay in touch with them. Cisco Systems's (Fortune #58) home page says, "See it. Live it. Share it."

Organizations have gone from closed, supersecret modes using skunkworks for innovation to strategies and methods that benefit from alliances and the benefits employees can provide when they have a better idea of what's going on around them. Don Tapscott, coauthor of *The Naked Corporation: How the Age of Transparency Will Revolutionize Business*[14] and *MacroWikinomics*,[15] says, " . . . openness [transparency] is not simply an obligation to report information to an external party like a regulator or an institutional investor; it's a new competitive force and an essential precondition for building productive relationships with stakeholders."[16]

Some of this sharing relies on collaboration tools. Socialtext chairman, president, and cofounder Ross Mayfield says:

> The big shift that we're seeing in organizations that are leveraging social software thoroughly is this shift from a need-to-know to a need-to-share culture; the ability to increase productivity by the way that you're coordinating your organization, in not just ways that are pre-subscribed, that are intelligently designed, but enabling them to emerge.[17]

Many of the examples Ross cites focus on the signaling capabilities that support the fast pace of internal activities and aid in keeping track of your brand and customers' needs. The organizations making the shift from a need-to-know approach to a need-to-share approach are agile and augment their formal hierarchy with information from outside. Knowledge flows more directly to where it is needed, and at less cost, to those with the answers—if you practice plugged-in management.

Yes, there is a need to share, but how do you help your organization gain the benefits without undue costs? When are Facebook, Twitter, email, or telephones OK at work? It depends on the technology (for example, security, available bandwidth), the organization (does this sharing disrupt others' work?), and people (can employees help the firm with their personal networks; are the employees able to make good decisions about their use of time?). Plugged-in managers may help groups work to find good practices that benefit all. Clearly a worse outcome is ignoring how new social network and communication affect ways of working.

Online retailer Zappos exemplifies the shift from need-to-know to need-to-share, and its people continue to find new ways to share how they do what they do. They have their formal sharing process via the ZapposInsights.com community (some free, some for a fee). You can attend classes, take a free tour, and interact with Zappos experts. They also have broad outreach like all-hands meetings and CEO Tony Hsieh's book *Delivering Happiness*.[18]

Zappos isn't the first to do this. Disney opened its Institute in 1986 to share Disney's approach to business strategy and how to treat "guests."[19] In 1987 the U.S. Congress created the Malcolm Baldrige National Quality Awards—with a requirement that winners share with others the story of how they have achieved their success. Though Zappos may not be the first, they are impressive in how they mix a variety of approaches together into a solid platform. They are taking full advantage of all the communication modes available to them, and they are not afraid of practicing, even delivering, transparency to the world.

Internal Transparency

The Zappos example illustrates some ways to share outside the organization's boundaries. Transparency within organizations is another environmental change that provides opportunities to plug in. Transparency has always been an important management topic (how much, with whom, about what). But we're now entering an era when transparency may have a chance of going mainstream. Three big triggers for that conclusion are:

- Comments by Socialtext CEO Eugene Lee suggesting that he's seeing greater transparency in a variety of firms. He gets to be on the front lines, as some of these companies are seeking out Socialtext products to help them manage their internal transparency.
- A wave of new books, such as *Transparency: How Leaders Create a Culture of Candor*[20] and *The New How: Creating Business Solutions Through Collaborative Strategy.*[21]
- A series of comments from blue chip companies at the 2009 and 2010 Enterprise 2.0 conferences, all with the theme "Social media creates transparency, often whether you want it or not—so you better manage it."

The New How

In *The New How*, Nilofer Merchant provides clear examples (often personal) of the flaws of top-down thinking and how a top-down approach threatens strategy development and implementation. The "Air Sandwich" she describes is a clear and memorable way to describe the problem of a lack of transparency:

> An Air Sandwich is, in effect, a strategy that has clear vision and future direction on the top layer, day-to-day action on

the bottom, and virtually nothing in the middle—no meaty key decisions that connect the two layers, no rich chewy center filling to align the new direction with new actions within the company.[22]

Transparency is one aspect of plugged-in management that can help us find the rich chewy center. "Everyone is better off when they know why decisions are made with as much accuracy as possible," Nilofer says.

It gives them an understanding of what matters and provides information on which to base the trade-offs constantly being made at every level. It also boosts buy-in and energy from the organization. When reasons behind decisions are not shared, the decisions can seem arbitrary and possibly self-serving. That is, they may seem like they are made for the good of the decision makers, rather than the good of the organization.[23]

As I watched Nilofer at a recent presentation, I noticed a logo on the audience-facing portion of her laptop: "co-create." This isn't transparency to be nice. This is transparency so that you can increase the chances you will create something significant.

Although management gurus have been pushing participative management forever, these new formulations of the ideas and our current technology environment may contain the levers that finally make transparency happen on a grand scale. In prior times management had to decide to practice transparency (for example, the weekly "huddle" described in Stack and Burlingham's 1992 book *The Great Game of Business*),[24] but with blogging, social media, and greater access to data, employees can create some of their own transparency.

World-renowned business school professor Warren Bennis and his coauthors offer evidence that transparency supports financial success. "Again and again, studies show that companies that rate high in transparency tend to outperform more opaque ones."[25] He cites a 2005 study finding that the stock performance of a group of twenty-seven U.S. companies noted as "most transparent" beat the S&P 500 by 11.3 percent.

Technology is transforming transparency in organizations of all sizes and types, not just Silicon Valley start-ups. My favorite quote during the 2009 Enterprise 2.0 conference came from Bryce Williams of Eli Lilly: "Culture can lead, so you better find tech ways that work for company goals." Translated into the language of plugged-in management, people are going to use technology to create their own transparency. You need to work with your colleagues to design technology tools and uses along with organizational processes to turn these efforts into organizational benefits. You should see transparency as an opportunity rather than a challenge. A well-informed organization is better able to perform on every level.

How to create a well-informed organization, rather than an information-overloaded rumor mill that leaks intellectual property, is a task for the plugged-in manager.

The Do-It-Ourselves (DIO) Economy

The transparency shift is well under way. However, there is another systemic shift building momentum, and this one may be even more dramatic in the long run. As *Wired* magazine editor-in-chief Chris Anderson presents it:

> Here's the history of two decades in one sentence: If the past 10 years have been about discovering post-institutional social models on the Web, then the next 10 years will be about applying them to the real world.
>
> This story is about the next 10 years.
>
> Transformative change happens when industries democratize, when they're ripped from the sole domain of companies,

governments, and other institutions and handed over to
regular folks. The Internet democratized publishing,
broadcasting, and communications, and the consequence
was a massive increase in the range of both participation
and participants in everything digital—the long tail of bits.[26]

Plugged-in managers need to understand the possibilities of
this new industrial revolution. Chris Anderson and others have
focused on DIY (do it yourself), but it's more than that. I see this
new approach as DIO (do it ourselves). Anderson does not tell
stories of lone inventors. Each of his examples highlights the
value of collaboration. If manufacturing tools and collaborative
design platforms continue to improve, there could be a new
industrial revolution.

A new industrial revolution will need plugged-in managers to
build the new organizational forms. Especially for knowledge
work, these new organizations may be even more virtual than
today's. They may be virtual over both distance and time, in that
they are made up of people from all over the world, who may
come together and then disperse as the work comes and goes.
These organizations may have more porous boundaries, with the
players coming and going to meet the needs of different projects.
Some of these shifts are enabled by technology tools that support
specific organizational practices. A basic list: recruiting, knowledge, evaluation, tools, and marketing.

Take the example of the website BuildItWith.Me, which con-
nects app designers and developers in the following areas of
expertise to "help you bootstrap your ideas into actual apps."[27]

Recruiting

Build It With Me supports innovation through both knowledge
and labor. You may be able to find someone with a skill you don't
have, but need, for your innovation—or you may be able to find
someone to just share the workload. The key is that you find them
by skill or interest rather than location or ad hoc connections.

Knowledge

Not everyone who helps you with your innovation has to be a member of the team. Communities of practice have always shared knowledge amongst their members. Knowledge sharing is one of their hallmarks. Internet versions of communities of practice increase the reach, speed, and ease of the process. For example, the Experimental Aircraft Association's Homebuilders' Corner was part of their 1953 newsletter. Through the wonders of the Internet you not only can find that 1953 information, but also, of course, have access to the current 24/7 searchable discussion-board version of Homebuilders' Corner.

Evaluation

Not all ideas are good ones. Many innovation support systems allow people to rate the idea, point out aspects of the project that may have already been done, and so forth. Cisco used a hybrid social networking approach in its I-Prize. The I-Prize was an open innovation prize competition, but the early stages were evaluated by the community. Intuit's Brainstorm tool similarly provides a hybrid approach offering evaluation and more (recruiting, work-flow support, and so on) across either an internal audience or one that crosses organizational boundaries.

Tools

In this instance, when I say tools, I mean real, touch-it-with-your-hands tools: lasers, saws, 3D printers.

Technically the tools themselves aren't Internet tools, but the connection is there in that members collaborate and share knowledge via the TechShop Members Forum. Other examples of Internet-based tools are more straightforward (for example, open source software), but not as likely to throw off sparks.

Marketing

One of the keys to user innovation (as opposed to closed corporate innovation) is that it be able to compete.[28] Software/web innovation has it easy in that transportation costs are virtually nil, but all innovations can take advantage of social media to gain immense marketing reach for little to no money.

• •

Recruiting, knowledge, evaluation, tools, and *marketing.* The Internet provides us with collaborative avenues toward innovation. Not all of these approaches are good for all organizations all the time. In fact, for your own organization the benefits may be rare. Still, plugged-in managers will pull from these capabilities to fit the needs of their organizations. A plugged-in manager is aware of the options and can justify the choices made, based on the rich setting of the manager's own organization.

The changes in technology, organizations, and people plus systemic shifts point to the value of plugged-in management within and across organizations. So what's a manager to do? First, we'll take a look at a case to illustrate plugged-in management in action. Let's see how Socialtext's Eugene Lee plugged in to his organization.

Eugene Lee's First Ninety Days at Socialtext

Socialtext is both a user and provider of enterprise collaboration tools. The company is a small, largely virtual organization, yet it has quickly become a preeminent provider of tools and services to other companies—and an icon of modern organizational design.

Many management books suggest that you have structured interviews with your direct reports when you join a new organization.[29] Eugene Lee followed this advice when he became CEO 2.0 for the collaboration/Enterprise 2.0 platform provider Socialtext. ("CEO 2.0" is how Ross Mayfield, Socialtext cofounder, advertised the job on LinkedIn). Eugene wrote down a set of questions like these:

- How long have you been here
- What are you most proud of in your career so far
- What will you be most proud of having done when you leave Socialtext?

What's unique is how this process evolved. Eugene had scheduled these one-on-one meetings for thirty minutes each and knew that wasn't much time for people to be thoughtful about their responses—so he posted the list of questions to the company wiki (a website where everyone in the company can post and edit information—it's also one of Socialtext's main products). The idea was to give people a chance to think about the questions before their face-to-face meetings. Eugene didn't anticipate that people would just start answering via the wiki—although that was predictable, given the company's culture and comfort with social software like this wiki.

Part of the picture is that Eugene hadn't come from companies with this kind of transparency. In fact, few companies today are comfortable with public posts and discussions of the sort found on wikis and blogs, and I'm guessing that during Eugene's tenure Cisco and Adobe weren't either.[30] This public response was a surprise to Eugene: unanticipated and somewhat unnerving (though he notes that the Socialtext employees wouldn't have thought of doing it any other way). But here's the key: Eugene is plugged in and quickly saw the value of the approach. He didn't post a recall to his email right away. He certainly didn't delete entries to the wiki. Instead, he added his own responses.

The wiki material ended up being the source material for his vision statement—especially the question, "What will you be most proud of having done when you leave?" Eugene also observed another dynamic: As people were contributing their thoughts, others were "gardening the wiki"—making it a well-designed document. The whole process became something Eugene described as "Getting to Know You 2.0." Sounds like a beautiful Silicon Valley leadership story.

At the time, it felt "so scary," Eugene said. "I'd lost control of the process." At the same time, he saw "how powerful it was to let that control go." With that level of collaboration and sharing of control, he said, "When you hit a tough spot and need people to do something hard . . . the trust is enormous." The software that Socialtext makes promotes that trust.

As a result, Eugene prepared an all-hands presentation covering "memes, themes, dreams, and seams"—what was common, what the aspirations were, and where there were gaps. Getting to Know You 2.0 was a success. It was a combination of technology (the Socialtext platform), organization (a way of working that assumed openness and transparency), and people dimensions (Eugene's being accepting of risk, even at this critical juncture with the new company; the Socialtext employees' initiative to begin sharing their answers). That's *plugged-in management*.

This was 2007. Jump forward to the middle of 2009. Eugene was given a copy of Bennis, Goleman, and O'Toole's book *Transparency: How Leaders Create a Culture of Candor.*[31] This book, and his Getting to Know You 2.0 story, have become part of how he presents Socialtext's products to other senior leaders.

As Eugene's story illustrates, plugged-in management is supported by trust, transparency, and a willingness to be flexible within a given situation. You need to be plugged in, given the increased complexities we're seeing within people, technology, and organization processes. However, it is unrealistic to think that, even if you are plugged in, you can predict all the outcomes. You can use plugged-in management to make the best predictions you can, but then you need to stay plugged in to be agile and effective in dealing with what actually occurs. In Part Two, I will explain in detail three key practices that plugged-in managers employ.

The Three Practices of the Plugged-In Manager

M y goal up to this point was to introduce the concept of plugged-in management and create a sense of how urgently it is needed today. Technology tools, organizational processes, and even the people of our organizations are changing in ways that require a thoughtful redesign of our approaches. There are also systemic shifts in terms of how communication and relationships cross formal organizational boundaries. You need to be plugged in to navigate this environment.

In Part One I show how to get plugged in by adding or emphasizing three particular practices in your management approach:

1. Scanning for choices across the people, technology, and organization dimensions of workplace decisions—what I call *Stop-Look-Listen*
2. Creatively blending those choices into effective strategies and tactics—*Mixing*

3. *Sharing*—ensuring that others understand your plugged-in approach and can work in parallel

Let's start with a short example from Internet retailer Zappos. I have dug into the history of the company, had the chance to take one of their famous tours, and corresponded with several Zappos Family members.[1] Zappos clearly developed their abilities to plug in as they built and developed their company. When you apply the ideas of plugged-in management from the ground up, the result is, in Zappos's words, "Wow!"

Wow! From the Fulfillment Center?

Founded in 1999, in 2010 Zappos was listed as the fifteenth best U.S. company to work for[2] and the number one ranked online retailer for customer service.[3] This is after a US$1.2 billion acquisition by Amazon—an acquisition that repaid years of personal investment and risk by early investors and employees. Zappos is a company built on providing Wow! Service (their term). If you look closely at Zappos, you can see Wow! supported by the three practices of plugged-in management at every level, in every dimension, from their website design to their fulfillment center.

Wow! from the fulfillment center? You don't think Zappos hits its Wow! service standard by drop shipping, do you? (Drop shipping is the common mail-order practice whereby orders are taken by the retailer, but then are sent to the manufacturing company, which then sends the order to the customer.) Zappos did start out that way, but drop shipping didn't give them the kind of control they needed to provide their extreme form of customer service. Though the team didn't have experience in complex inventory systems, they jumped in, got their hands dirty, and created a system to hit their service goals while still managing costs. The iterations they've gone through show deep abilities to plug in, driven by their focus on delivering a Wow! experience to their customers—as well as great shoes and other products.

Take it from Keith Glynn, the guy who jumped on a plane to Kentucky, without going home to pack, to help for a couple of weeks with third-party warehouse issues—and ended up staying for two years.[4] At the point where Keith and Zappos CEO Tony Hsieh decided they needed to run their own warehouse, Keith went back to San Francisco to pick up his truck. He and Tony then drove the truck for thirty-six hours nonstop to Kentucky. This is serious commitment to warehouse operations!

I asked Keith how Zappos came to run the fulfillment center the way they do.[5] I'd read that they randomly stocked the shoes, as this actually made things easier to find![6] Keith's response:

> In a traditional brick and mortar store stocking was done based on Brand, Style, Size and Color. At Zappos originally there was no intent to stock inventory. As Zappos grew we realized we wanted to own the customer experience, so we started to hold inventory.
>
> We started with a small space in our office. It held a couple thousand pairs of shoes. This consisted of static racking and the shoes were stocked based on what other stores were doing. Brand, Style, Size, Color. We learned early on that this was a laborious job. You would have to continually shift brands because you did not account for seasonality and future growth.[7]

In 2000, Zappos moved to a larger warehouse in Willows, California. As Keith tells it:

> We would receive a shipment, let's say from UGG. We would have to unbox the shoes. Lay them out in a large area on the floor based on style, size and color. Imagine hundreds of shoe boxes laid out on the floor and the amount of space needed to do this. And this was only one brand.

Once you had them organized you would have to now figure out how to put them on the racks for storage. In order to get everything to fit you most likely had to shift thousands of shoes to get everything in the proper place. There were other brands on each side which had to be moved as well. We would review our processes and come up with some small wins as to efficiency but it could cost us in space or other areas. We thought it would be great to have a system where we did not have to rotate the inventory every day when the shipments came in. We had the idea but did not have the resources or know how to make it work.

In 2002, they thought they had a solution when warehouse service provider eLogistics offered to take over the warehouse and fulfillment operations. eLogistics had a warehouse next to the UPS Worldport hub; this would speed up shipping. "When we moved to the Kentucky eLogistics location they did things quite differently," Keith told me.

They had large static racks about twenty-five to thirty feet high. This probably worked for most of what they were shipping but there was no way it would work for us. We had large volumes of shoes, thousands of SKUs [stock keeping units—product identifiers]. The need for speed and accuracy was extremely important to us as this was our business' "customer service."

We had many conversations with eLogistics on how to improve what they were doing. We even had them install shorter racks so it wouldn't take as long to put shoes away or pick for shipping. They only wanted to use this space for the faster moving products and felt the need to grow upward since this space was available to them. Imagine having thirty-foot ceilings and only six-foot racks. I could see their rationale but it would not work for Zappos. Another challenge was that we were paying them for space. Basically this was a cube that varied in size. Let's say one

foot long by two feet wide by eighteen inches deep. They
may have had only one or two shoes in the space based on
Brand, Style, Size or Color that we had in inventory. This left
a lot of empty space that we were paying for since we paid
for the entire cube.

This is the sort of problem that requires serious plugged-in
management skills. At this point they are trying to work with
building space, types of storage racks, costs, alliance partners,
customer perception, and human heights (note the comment
about shorter racks and stocking). You can see how the team is
stopping, looking, listening as they scan for the best option.

They eventually decided to again have their own warehouse.
Keith went shopping for a warehouse and found one only fifteen
minutes from the Louisville airport. Again, good for shipping and
thus for customer service.[8] They signed the lease and took the
crazy road trip mentioned above in preparation for moving the
inventory.

In *Delivering Happiness,* Tony Hsieh tells the story of how they
gave eLogistics a last chance to keep the business.[9] They designed
a competition pitting Zappos's new warehouse operations against
that of eLogistics. For every week that the Zappos system beat
eLogistics on shipping and inventory accuracy, ten thousand pairs
of shoes would move from the eLogistics warehouse to the new
Zappos warehouse. It took only a month for the Zappos warehouse to win all the inventory. "It was a valuable lesson," Hsieh
says. "We learned that we should never outsource our core competency. As an e-commerce company, we should have considered
warehousing to be our core competency from the beginning."[10]

Keith continues:

While receiving the inventory, Tony came up with a quick
program that would allow us to scan the UPCs [the
"universal product code" you see with a barcode on many
products] into a location on a shelf. This allowed us to put

any shoe anywhere in the racks and we would be able to
find it based on the UPC and the rack location. We realized
that this system would give us a higher density of storage
and allow us to store items randomly.

Random storage is good for the people in the warehouse. The
inventory system lets the worker know where to find the box, and
because it's randomly stored, the specific box the worker is looking
for will stand out among different brands and styles. Think about
having to grab the right box if it were stored next to boxes
that all were identical except for a color or size designation.
Random brand storage works better in concert with the inventory
system, as the boxes are more distinctive.

But Zappos needed yet another innovation. UPCs are not
unique to a particular pair of shoes. That is, the pair of size 7
Chocolate Leather Fitflops that *I* bought would have the same
UPC code as the pair of size 7 Chocolate Leather Fitflops that *you*
bought. No good for managing inventory or returns. In addition,
some boxes have multiple UPCs printed on them. The warehouse
team needed a unique identifier for each and every unique box
of shoes.

The LPN (license plate number) system they came up with
turns out to be an excellent example of plugged-in management
in action. It's a great way for Zappos to track the location of every
item accurately in the warehouse and have a higher density of
storage—the technology component. They are able to track specific items through receiving, shipping, and returns. (Fun fact:
One out of every sixty overnight packages shipped by UPS is a
Zappos box!)[11] As a result, they are able to be amazingly responsive to customer service needs (and so be true to the Zappos Wow!
standard of service)—that's technology and organizational
process. Random storage takes into account human perception—
that's people. It's the mixing of these dimensions that makes the
LPN system so powerful. All from a number!

The Zappos Family is also strongly focused on the third practice of plugged-in managers: sharing. I was able to correspond with Keith and his colleagues because of Zappos's openness, its proclivity for sharing. Tony Hsieh says in the preface to *Delivering Happiness*, "I decided to write this book to help people avoid making many of the same mistakes that I've made."[12] Through the Zappos Insights website, experiences, and community, the Zappos Family freely shares the "how" as well as the "what" of their company.[13]

As the Zappos.com case study demonstrates, plugged-in management works for individuals, groups, organizations, and cross-organization relationships. When we talk about the people, technology, and organizations of plugged-in management, think about all of the different levels where plugging in can help you thrive.

First Practice: Stop-Look-Listen

S top-Look-Listen is the first practice of the plugged-in manager. Sounds like three practices, but you need to roll them into one. You no doubt learned the basics of the Stop-Look-Listen practice as a child learning to cross the street or a train track. Now we can use it for assessing the roles that people, technology, and organizational process play in a particular organizational environment. Just as you wouldn't want your child to do only one of the steps before crossing the street, you don't want to do only one of the steps in your work.

Stop-Look-Listen means to evaluate the people, technology, and organization process opportunities or challenges present in your particular environment. Consider the American Society for Testing and Materials (ASTM) International, an organization that supports the development and archiving of high-quality, market-relevant standards, beginning with a standard established in 1901 for railway steel. (These are standards like the ones you see quoted on items from airplane parts to baby strollers: something like "meets ASTM standard F833.") In the 1990s, the management of ASTM stopped to consider their environment as they looked ahead and saw the Internet and electronic communication as a possible track for improvement on their ninety years of success.

ASTM saw that the Internet and new forms of communication (ubiquitous email and access to Internet-based tools like discussion boards, videoconferencing, and voting) would provide an innovative foundation for how they do their job. They understood that to take advantage of this new technology, they would need to adjust their formal organizational process for engaging a broad spectrum of stakeholders. It's critical to understand that ASTM standards are not handed down from management on high. Not at all. Standards—at least those developed via ASTM's process—are a community effort created explicitly via a "balanced" process in which all stakeholders are heard and decisions are made by a fair and transparent ballot process.

ASTM's Dan Schultz explained how they came to their new approach:

> Walking into the mid-90s [during the early growth of the Internet] with ninety years of experience, [ASTM] knew exactly what it had to do. . . . In order to maintain commercial advantage, the standards development of tomorrow has to develop the most technically competent standard in the shortest amount of time or the industry won't select you.[1]

He described how ASTM formally sketched out the new digital path for "cradle to grave standards development." They made sure that their products—standards—could be created quickly, be easily accessible, and be in a form that the customer wanted. They made sure that their process was improved by the use of electronic collaboration. They haven't replaced face-to-face collaboration;

rather, they have streamlined those face-to-face meetings with their new pre- and post-meeting processes.

Assessing the Environment

ASTM got onto the path to an Internet-enabled process by first carefully assessing the changing environment, rather than rushing in. They stopped, they looked, and they listened.

In the sections that follow I highlight the Stop-Look-Listen process, using examples from a variety of organizations. The basic idea is to:

- Reflect and consider the options—stop.
- Find or create data to help you make your decisions—look.
- Because it's unlikely that your first effort will be perfect, build in feedback mechanisms—listen.

Stop

The ASTM example just detailed emphasizes the value of stopping for conscious reflection. By consciously stopping to reflect, we prevent ourselves from reinventing the wheel. Stopping also allows us to prioritize. Most research into change suggests taking "small bites" that let us easily track outcomes along the way.[2] If you stop and prioritize, you can pick initial activities where you have the most room for improvement—and the least room for loss.

It's not an accident that the Six Sigma quality improvement movement uses martial arts language to describe the expertise levels of its practitioners: Green belts understand the basics; black belts are experts and leaders, and they can teach others. One of the philosophical connections between the Six Sigma approach and martial arts is the importance of heightening your state of consciousness related to your practice. For martial arts this is consciousness of your surroundings and your skill levels and those of your opponents, and a systematic understanding of the likely outcomes of your specific actions. The same applies to conscious reflection in organizational settings as well.

Gianna Clark, vice president of customer service at Dominion Virginia Power, was a longtime contributor to iSixSigma, a community website providing resources to Six Sigma practitioners. In a humorous response to widespread, but perhaps not well-informed, critiques of the Six Sigma approach, she said:

> Let's see, define the problem, measure it, analyze data to develop solutions, improve the process and make sure the improvement sticks. Sounds like a good approach to me. Maybe it's the execution. Selecting a project that supports corporate objectives, using a cross-functional team made up of process experts and gathering input from the customer. Nope—no issues here. Right then, maybe it's the data driven decision-making or the methodology's ability to fix long-standing problems. No—not a problem either.[3]

Gianna Clark is outlining the benefit of stopping to have thoughtful, conscious reflection around organizational action. Problem definition, measurement techniques, and analysis are conscious efforts applied in particular settings. Plugged-in managers will stop and reflect on the options across available technology, organizational practices, and the human context.

There is support in general management research for stopping and being conscious of your whole system. For example, Marlena Fiol and Edward O'Connor are experts on mindful managers. In their 2003 research, they show that mindful managers think about their situations in terms of rich categories, are open to new information, and are aware that there are always multiple perspectives.[4] These managers are conscious of their situation and the choices that they make. This more conscious approach to management practice can lead to broader environmental scanning so that more and better information is gathered, resulting in more precise contextual interpretations of the situation and, ultimately, more discriminating decisions. This leads us to the next step: look.

Look

Just as the Look step makes sure a child looks in both directions for oncoming traffic before crossing a street, this step reminds us to use available data, observation, and simple experiments to identify opportunities from various vantage points.

Google's publicly stated mission is to "organize the world's information and make it universally accessible and useful,"[5] but they also occasionally give specifics of what to do with that information. For example, Google's Marissa Mayer, vice president of location and local services, often speaks on the value of data and experiments for business decision making. In her description of how information helps Google build better products, she gave a clear example in terms of the testing that led to the particular shade of blue used in their links.[6]

Yes, Google stops and looks before making decisions about things that seem as trivial as the shade of blue used in the links provided on their web pages. Apparently the links on the Google Search site were a different shade of blue from the links on the Gmail site. The Google designers wanted the sites to be the same but also wanted to make an informed decision. They wanted to *look*.

Their experiment randomly divided all Google users into forty different groups. Each group saw one of forty different shades of blue links for two weeks. At the end of the two weeks, Google analyzed the results in terms of number of click-throughs (the rate at which Google users clicked on a link). It turned out that the more greenish a blue link is, the less likely users are to click on the link. As of this writing, if you take a look at the Google

Search and Gmail sites, you'll see a distinctively blue color to the links.

This is an example of how a company can use internal experiments to come to a plugged-in decision. The Google engineers know that they can change the technology of their websites to learn about people's behavior. They have organizational practices and norms in place that support their use of experiments to make decisions. Modern technology gives us much easier access to data than in the past, but we have to stop and look before this information can provide value. At Google, there is a culture of data and evidence that supports this plugged-in practice. It is clear in Google's organizational norm for the experimentation described by Marissa Mayer.

Google has created an organizational climate in which the expectation is that employees and management will stop and look—and that when it comes to decision making, the business outcomes of this process will be more important than individual outcomes. This is a perfect environment for plugged-in management to yield enviable outcomes. As a Google employee, you are expected to have a framework for your decision making and are given the tools and resources to use the framework. Google management appears to understand that conscious use of plugged-in management practices will lead to better business outcomes because the process will be better informed about the environment that the business is working in.

Listen

Knowing your environment also means being willing to listen to others. Plugged-in management acknowledges the dynamic nature of your use of technology tools, organizational processes, and people's changing skills and needs. You can use feedback from others to help you decide whether to continue to focus on the initial path or to move on to a different one.

A while back, I had the pleasure of spending the day with folks from SRI International (a large research group founded in 1946 by Stanford University), the U.S. Army, PARC (an R&D company, originally part of Xerox), and some other interesting organizations. Much of the discussion focused on the organizational practice of After Action Reviews (AARs). An AAR is a structured feedback process that considers intended goals, actual outcomes, and opportunities for improvement.

We were specifically interested in AARs in a world where social media and social networks play a major role in communication. The best AARs will take place immediately after the activity, regardless of a good or bad outcome, and involve as many of the players as possible. Social media and networks create more opportunities for using AARs and can keep the process top of mind— the idea is to go where your audience already is. If your audience is on a social media site like Facebook, Twitter, or the organization's private system, there are opportunities to integrate those tools with the AAR practice.

The U.S. Army is credited with the modern form of the AAR and offers a simple set of questions to guide the review:[7]

1. What did we set out to do?
2. What happened?
3. Why did it happen?
4. What are we going to do about it?

LTC Nate Allen, one of the two founders of the Army's well-received early efforts in social media,[8] reported some updates on their AAR process: They are finding good value in comparing "close calls" with bad outcomes. Close calls don't get people as defensive as they would be with a disaster—this is the better learning environment. They also now include another agenda item: What did we get away with? For example, the outcome was OK, but in hindsight there could have been a problem, and this possibility should be considered in the review.

Overall, one of the benefits of doing AARs as a matter of course is that it may be less likely that emotions cloud the evaluation process if it's a standard tool and the approach is familiar. Also, calling it a "review" rather than a "postmortem" (a term much more common in U.S. organizations) implies that the AAR focuses on a process that is alive, not dead and done.

Thinking in plugged-in management terms, AARs give you windows of opportunity to listen and take action to improve the people, technology, and organization mix you develop in the next steps of your plugged-in process. To the extent that you can use technology such as social media to support the AAR or similar approach, it is more likely to be a living process (for example, by tracking the workflow in the first place, so the AAR can be evidence-based, or by capturing the outcomes of the AAR, so that the determined changes can be tracked and themselves evaluated).

It is critical to see AARs as a process, not an outcome. You don't do an AAR to generate content (for example, lessons learned)—though that can be a great outcome. You do an AAR to carefully reflect on what could be done better to help you consciously plan for the future.

Proactive Listening

The participants in an AAR-like feedback activity are critical sources of information for the review. The AAR process must be thoughtfully integrated into an overall system of feedback and not be individual performance reviews or scapegoating. The information gained from listening is likely to be biased without these boundaries.

You should also listen to feedback from outside your organization's walls. Seesmic, one of the top software tools for managing social media communications for Twitter and Facebook, provides a good example. Seesmic CEO Loic Le Meur focuses on the business value of social media in his interview for the Ideas Project. (The Nokia-sponsored Ideas Project website is a community home for "big ideas" around the future of communications and technology.) He opens with descriptions of how sharing changes everything—diffusing your ideas, as opposed to protecting them—and then addresses the value of sharing ideas with social media friends and how this gives you instant access to their thinking:

> It has already changed the way I think. I feel like I live in a room, which is across the world, but I can just call a friend and there will always be someone to answer one of my questions, as long as I share as well with them. It's two ways. It's about living in a world with a community that can help you . . .
>
> It changed me completely. I cannot think alone anymore. I need to think with my friends, all the time.[9]

Loic Le Meur uses technology (social media) to gain easy access to feedback from outside his organization's walls, but he clearly understands that he must reciprocate to participate in these forums. He uses social media to facilitate his listening, but he also realizes that the technology is part of an overall ecosystem with specific norms.

Plugged-in managers also listen in a more formal sense. While the Lockheed Skunk Works and Apple are known for their secrecy, many organizations now open up their research and development processes so that outsiders can participate. This is more than "open innovation," wherein organizations are willing to look for innovation to buy or license from other organizations.[10] This is public, interactive innovation with an open community of users and other interested participants. Some examples of corporate self-representations:

- IDEO Labs: ". . . is a place where we can show bits of what we're working on, talk about prototyping, and share our excitement over the tools that help us create."[11]
- Google Labs: "Explore Google's technology playground."[12]
- PARC Living Laboratory: "In the spirit of open innovation, this is one of the places where PARC scientists and engineers share their prototype web-based services, alpha-stage software downloads, proof-of-concept for various competencies, and collaborative development programs. These are available free to the public for trial and feedback; in turn, we hope to draw on the diverse perspectives the online community will share."[13]
- NASA Innovation Incubator: "New partnerships to: Engage private citizens in aerospace technology development, bring fresh ideas into NASA, help emerging technologies reach maturity, promote the growth of a competitive space industry."[14]
- LotusLive Labs: "LotusLive Labs provides you with the opportunity to experience and evaluate pre-alpha innovations from LotusLive . . . You're invited to explore and provide feedback on these new cloud-based technologies designed for your business. Who knows, your input could help us shape the next great features from LotusLive!"[15]
- My Starbucks Idea: "You know better than anyone else what you want from Starbucks. So tell us. What's your Starbucks Idea? Revolutionary or simple—we want to hear it. Share your ideas, tell us what you think of other people's ideas and join the discussion. We're here, and we're ready to make ideas happen. Let's get started."[16]
- U.S. Government Grand Challenges of the 21st Century: "Today, the Office of Science and Technology Policy and the National Economic Council are releasing a 'request for information' that is designed to collect input from the

public regarding: The grand challenges that were identified
in the President's innovation strategy . . . Partners (e.g.
companies, investors, foundations, social enterprises, non-
profit organizations, philanthropists, research universities,
consortia, etc.) that are interested in collaborating with each
other and the Administration to achieve one or more of
these goals; and Models for creating an 'architecture of
participation' that allows many individuals and organizations
to contribute to the process of finding solutions to these
grand challenges."[17]

These sites provide the hosting organizations with early and
ongoing feedback from enthusiastic followers. This is participative listening that can give them deep insight into their broader
organizational environment.

How Do Plugged-In Managers Decide How Open to Be?

How do you decide what to be open with and what to keep secret?
Technology allows you to be open, but the plugged-in management approach pushes for considering the organizational implications. Hank Chesbrough and David Teece provide a valuable
framework to help you with these decisions.[18] Their framework
has you consider whether or not the innovation already exists
(perhaps someone else has already been open with the innovation) or must be invented, and whether the innovation will be an
autonomous module or a fully integrated part of the organization's goals and processes.

Broadly speaking, you want to bring in-house innovations that
must be created (versus those that already exist) and that will be
fully integrated across the organization or its product. For
example, you don't see Google open-sourcing their search and ad
placement algorithms—these algorithms are their "secret sauce,"

in that they contain cutting-edge, internally invented methods that cut across their organizational capabilities. Instead, the things we see within Google Labs are user-facing tools for which Google is interested in early feedback about use patterns and experience. These innovations are more autonomous to the rest of Google's activities and are safe—and valuable—to share during their development.

The Perils of Not Listening

In an always-on, Internet-enabled world, not listening can mean that your organization sustains substantial damage before you can respond. In late 2009, B. L. Ochman, a digital media consultant, used her personal experience with Time Warner as the basis for a blog post, "Three Top Ways to Damage Your Brand With Social Media."[19] Ochman used Twitter to document her Time Warner cable service problems, posting to the Twitter account TimeWarnerCares. Noting that she had had no reply in twenty-four hours, she observed, "That's approximately one week in Internet time." This suggests that no one is listening at Time Warner. But there is more to this story.

First, some context: ComcastCares, the Twitter account originated by Comcast customer service manager Frank Eliason, is of huge value to Comcast, a Time Warner competitor. *BusinessWeek*'s Rebecca Reisner says,

> I think it's safe to call Comcast's Frank Eliason the most famous customer service manager in the U.S., possibly in the world. Ten months ago, Eliason, whose official title is director of digital care, came up with the idea of using Twitter to interact with customers of Comcast (CMCSA), the mammoth provider of cable TV, Internet, and phone services for whom he has worked for a year and a half.[20]

The twist in the Ochman story: Time Warner didn't own the TimeWarnerCares account (their current Twitter support address is TWCableHelp). Eventually the fact came out that TimeWarnerCares was an impostor, but the damage was already done.

B. L. Ochman reported on the error, and the resolution, once she was in touch with the right people.[21] But she stood by her point that Time Warner should have been looking for and listening to all the social media chatter from customers having problems.

Social media technologies with a broad reach are here. Plugged-in managers are aware of their audience (users, customers, employees, and more) and find ways to follow discussions relevant to their piece of the organization. Google, Twitter, Facebook, and your internal communication tools have search capabilities—and often, search capabilities that can be automated. Automated search can provide effective listening posts for gathering positive, negative, and future-looking feedback about your environment.

Now let's take a look at an organization that has been practicing plugged-in management for decades.

Providence Regional Medical Center

Plugged-in managers understand human, technical, and organizational opportunities, and they're able to mix them together to do exceptional things. The staff at Providence Regional Medical Center of Everett, Washington, practice plugged-in management on a broad scale.[22] Their examples are valuable because they give hope for health care innovation, they show us an exceptional process over a long span of years, and they help us see technology tools beyond computers and email. What's more, they exemplify the benefits of a conscious Stop-Look-Listen process.

Providence Regional had been an early innovator in fast-tracking routine cardiac surgical patients (for example, patients with scheduled bypass surgeries). Patients in the fast-track program would spend the night following surgery in the Cardiac Critical Care Unit and the next day be moved to a room in the "step-down" unit to begin monitored recovery and rehabilitation. This quick transition to rehabilitation supports faster recovery and shorter hospital stays. Twelve years ago this was an innovative and successful program, but as the hospital grew and the patient load increased, they began to see problems.

The hospital is "fairly proactive," said Chief Nursing Officer Kim Williams, in the way they manage patients and look at organizational processes. For example, she said, "We noticed that after the night shift nurse helped the patient up and the day shift nurse helped them to the room's recliner in preparation for transfer, sometimes a bed [in the step-down unit] wasn't immediately available."

Cardiac Critical Care staff nurse Judy Espedal explained:

> I was noticing that patients were staying in the recliner for four to six hours waiting for their bed. By the time they did get to their new room they were exhausted. The therapists assigned to them were gone for the day and patients weren't receiving respiratory, physical, or occupational therapy until the next morning thus missing out on twenty-four hours of care. We are Critical Care nurses, not physical therapists. We didn't have the practices built into our routines to get them moving [important for faster recovery]. We didn't have the tools to walk them—they were hooked to everything.

Around 2002, Judy had a hallway conversation with Dr. Jim Brevig, director of cardiac surgery. "They are missing a whole day," Judy told him. "By the time they get their new room, get in bed, and the new nurse assesses, it's 4 P.M. They are missing a whole day of walking and other therapy."

Dr. Brevig's response: "What can we do about this, Judy?"

"So that's when we started," Judy told me. "We formed a task force to brainstorm ways to get around this. 'Is there some way we can bring the care to the patient?'"

That's the origin of their Cardiac Surgery Single Stay Unit (CSSU). In a single stay unit, the patient stays in place while the care and equipment come to them. The nurses, patients, and families have a single location that is changed to meet the patient's needs. Kim Williams notes that they have portable x-rays, smart pumps (for medication), and telemetry units for each patient. As the patient improves, the staff moves the equipment out to make the room look like the patient is getting closer to home. Judy Espedal describes it as "family centered care."

They didn't implement this approach on a whim, but based it on data and more data. In other words, they stopped, looked, and listened. Before asking for a pilot program, Judy Espedal, Dr. Brevig, and representatives from hospital administration, the partner step-down unit, and respiratory therapy visited two hospitals that had implemented single stay units (though not for cardiac surgery). The team brought back impressions and outcome data from the other hospitals. Following the presentation of this material, Providence gave them two of the unit's beds and permission to pilot the single stay approach for three or four months. They brought in portable monitoring equipment to let them extend their capabilities and added training for the nurses in how to switch from critical to rehabilitative care as the patient's needs change.

Note that the team had to mix together people, technology, and organizational process: A single stay approach calls for technology that is portable and staff with a broad range of skills to manage the different stages of care. Although a facility can renovate to support the single stay, the Providence team found ways to work with what they had.[23] Kim Williams believes single stay can work in any room with a toilet (yes, room architecture is a technology!)—meaning most hospital rooms could be single stay rooms if the other technology and practice adjustments are viable.

Judy Espedal says patients and families are now working with the same critical care nurses from admission to discharge. When a nurse can focus on the same two patients over days, it allows for better care. "We can think of everything," Judy says. "We can get in an extra walk, sit with family . . . time to look at the whole picture." Dr. Brevig notes that information transfer across the team has also improved, given their twelve-hour shifts: The increased rapport, given contact time with patients and family, means that subtle, tacit knowledge transfers more accurately—and only one handoff takes place per day, rather than the two that would be required if the shifts were eight hours. There is less opportunity for critical information to be lost.

What is the result of Providence's ability to restructure based on technologies at hand, training to increase the breadth of nursing skills, and adjustments to patient care? Success. They decreased the time patients spend in the hospital by approximately a half-day, and they have earned 99 to 100 percent satisfaction ratings from patients and families and numerous awards for the unit, plus numerous requests to tell their story to other medical providers. Is this evidence of plugged-in management or just a lucky outcome? Given that they've made a variety of similar transformations over the years, the staff of Providence Regional Medical Center are clearly demonstrating full-on, team-level plugged-in management skill.

The experiences of the staff at Providence Regional Medical Center demonstrate that plugged-in management isn't just a soft skill—something that might be made fun of in a Dilbert cartoon. Plugged-in management is the systematic consideration of peoples' capabilities, organizational process, and technology (even in the form of a hospital room toilet). Plugged-in management can be an informal general approach to work or it can include a formal assessment strategy.

Stop-Look-Listen in Action

The Cardiac Surgery team has made not just one transformation, but several—each drawing on people, technology, and organizational practice to provide improvements in patient care. They don't explicitly talk about their approach in terms of Stop-Look-Listen, but the three steps are clearly visible in various examples.

Single Stay

Cardiac critical care nurse Judy Espedal stopped long enough to notice the length of time patients were waiting to be transferred to the step-down unit and brought it to the attention of the rest of the team. The cardiac team as a group is open to reflection—to noticing—and has programs in place to collect data about their environment. The value of their approach is supported by a much-quoted statement from the management literature: "Noticing may be at least as important as sensemaking. . . . If events are noticed, people make sense of them; and if events are not noticed, they are not available for sensemaking."[24]

Once the cardiac team members were aware of the problem, they were able to look carefully at the patient transfer issue. The team's looking took the form of visiting other hospitals to see how they were handling similar patient transfer issues. The cardiac team then used this information to take a plugged-in approach to designing Providence's own pilot cardiac single stay program. They used available and new technologies (in-room toilets, portable medical equipment) and new organizational practices (patients stay in one room with day and night cardiac care nurses and other rehabilitative experts supporting the full range of patient care), and they understood and supported patients' and families' needs to develop relationships with caregivers.

The pilot single stay program then allowed the team to listen for the results of their organizational and technological transformation. The team gathered solid feedback concerning the outcomes of the pilot program and tracked patient satisfaction ratings and length of stay. The benefits of 99 to 100 percent patient satisfaction and approximately a half-day reduction in patient length of stay led to making cardiac single stay a permanent and honored aspect of their patient care.

Blood Conservation

Another example of the Providence cardiac team's Stop-Look-Listen practice is the blood conservation program initiated by Dr. Jim Brevig, director of cardiac surgery, in 2004 (less transfused blood after cardiac surgery is better in many cases).[25]

The Stop step in this case was how Dr. Brevig stopped and reflected on the results he was seeing in his professional journals.

The Look step involved examining how these results from other hospitals could be applied to the Providence setting. With this understanding, Dr. Brevig worked with the team to build new practices for blood transfusion that intertwined technical and organizational changes and added to the training of the critical care nurses. He pushed for:

- Changes in bypass machine settings to reduce the use of transfused blood.
- Changes in surgical techniques to reduce blood loss.
- Addition of a blood conservation coordinator to the staff.
- Development of new nursing practices, whereby blood transfusions are based on patient outcomes rather than as a matter of routine, as dictated by prior training. Brevig worked directly with the critical care nurses to achieve this change.

The Listen step took the form of studying the differences in patient outcomes before and after the practice changes. The data verify the blood conservation program's success. From 2003 to

2007, the transfusion rate decreased from 43 percent to 18 percent, and the hospital stay time was reduced by a half-day.

Skilled Nursing Education in the Local Community

In a third example, the Stop step begins with the cardiac surgery team's routine assessment of readmission data. This routine practice enabled the team to notice changes or see opportunities for improvement.[26] Their conscious watching revealed a bump to 12.2 percent of patients being readmitted to the hospital within thirty days of their initial discharge.

The team used their technical statistical analysis expertise and broad understanding of clinical practices and patient behaviors to look deeply into the issues—even outside of their own organizational walls. They found that many of the readmitted patients were from skilled nursing facilities. Chief Nursing Officer Kim Williams says the team developed practices to help these local facilities be better prepared to take on patients after cardiac surgery. They created an education program in which a cardiac surgeon or critical care nurse team visits the skilled nursing facilities to help educate the staff. They teach the facility staff about the common problems associated with readmissions, at no charge to the skilled nursing facility.

In this example, too, the cardiac surgery team listened for the results of their transformation. In 2009, the readmission rate was down to 8.1 percent.

These are conscious, explicit applications of plugged-in management, from buy-in, to showing that an innovation works, through pilot tests, instituting the new practice, and ongoing evaluation. No single functional area within the team is making a decision. No single layer of the organization is making a decision. No single technology or organizational process stands above the rest. The cardiac surgery team takes a long-term perspective, working with their full system of opportunities, because plugged-in management is a long-term activity.

Is There Something Special About the Cardiac Surgical Team?

What enables this team to take such a distinctively different approach to problems so common in today's hospitals? Dr. Brevig's opinion is that the collaborative nature of Providence Regional overall pushes for buy-in and input from all members of the unit. In other words, Providence Regional has a broad organizational norm that supports their stopping, looking, and listening across all the stakeholders. This diversity is what supports its plugged-in practices. Consideration of human capabilities, technology tools, and organizational processes will all end up in the mix if a diverse set of stakeholders is involved in the discussion. Diversity in the group making design and problem solution decisions is more likely to engage people with both technical and organizational perspectives. Open discussion is also more likely to highlight the range of knowledge, skills, and abilities of the people to be involved in the transformations.

Cardiac care nurse Judy Espedal highlighted the team's second distinguishing feature: the time and focus needed to support their success. Their transformations take years, and the team has to apply itself resolutely from start to finish. Such a commitment to the long haul is more likely given the Providence environment: With collaboration and communication, commitment to projects is more likely across all kinds of organizations.[27]

An additional difference between the cardiac surgery team and many other teams and organizations is that the cardiac team actually does assess their environment. Many teams and organizations do not take that conscious step. The cardiac team is consciously aware of their environment and how it can be improved. Then their observational data appears to flow freely via collaboration, attention to communication, and long-term commitment.

The Value of Systematically Assessing the Environment

We all have plugged-in management skills, to the extent that we are able to see and understand human, technical, and organizational opportunities—and limitations—and make effective decisions about how to mix them together in a particular context. I see many people practicing plugged-in management on autopilot, but few do so consciously. Why is more conscious use better? When should you systematically assess your environment rather than just using plugged-in management skills on the fly?

The great scientist Louis Pasteur is credited with saying "Chance favors the prepared mind." Similarly, each of the examples in this chapter highlights the benefits of being aware of your environment and understanding your options as they develop. Awareness and conscious attention to the process result in more and better information about your environment, and in more and better attention to multiple perspectives on what to do with that information.

Consider our examples. ASTM stepped smoothly into the Internet age because they were paying attention to innovations that might streamline their workflow. Google sees great advantage, for themselves and all of us, in the power of extracting meaning from the vast information resources created through people's use of the Internet. The U.S. Army evaluates and looks for improvement both because they see value in continuous improvement and because they realize their environment is likely to change. Seesmic CEO Loic Le Meur can't imagine working in a world cut off from quick feedback from his environment, and the Time Warner Cable story provides a counterpoint: the result of not looking in today's hyperconnected world. A variety of organizations are opening up their R&D both to directly gain feedback and to be engaged with their stakeholders in changing environments. Finally, the cardiac surgery team shows us how being aware of your environment can have long-term, life-saving benefits.

The first practice of plugged-in management is to understand the possibilities and pitfalls across your people, technology, and organization environments. In other words, capture the ongoing benefit of the childhood refrain: Stop-Look-Listen. Knowing your environment and the available building blocks of technology tools, organizational processes, and the people involved provides you with the raw materials to effectively accomplish a needed change. The next step is to learn to mix these raw materials for powerful outcomes.

chapter
FOUR

Second Practice: Mixing

You've stopped. You've looked. You've listened. Now that you can see the people, technology, and organization possibilities in the environment, how do you put them together and follow through with implementation?

Mixing is the second practice of the plugged-in manager.

Mixing is a metaphor for how you bring together the people possibilities, the technology possibilities, and the organizational possibilities to create a way of working. You can't just make a change to one of these three dimensions without making a balancing adjustment to the others. Think about making a rich stew. If you add more stock, you may need to add more seasoning, given the dilution, or you could choose to just let the mixture cook down and reconcentrate the flavors through evaporation.

I've used the term "weaving" a lot in the past to describe how to bring together technology tools, organizational processes, and people in a balanced way. But I think the idea of mixing is better in that it makes clear that the individual ingredients combine, to a degree, versus just being intertwined. The problem with weaving as an analogy is that it allows the component parts to remain independent. Take a look at the cloth you're wearing. Each of the threads is intertwined with others, but they are not mixed together. With mixing you are not only balancing the technology tools, organizational practices, and human aspects, but also blending them to a degree. For example, as people gain experience with particular tools and practices, their knowledge, skills, and abilities will expand and their motivations to use particular approaches may be influenced positively or negatively.

Consider the internal wiki described in Chapter Two. Socialtext uses these user-editable websites as ways of collaborating on documents within their organization. Using a wiki rather than email with attachments generally requires the technical implementation of a wiki tool, a shift in company practices to say that the wiki will be the home for collaboration on documents and that email use should be reduced, and some education in both the tool and the practice (learning, for example, how you log into the tool, or when it is or isn't appropriate to change something someone else has written). As people gain experience with the wiki, they may find new uses and shift the way they do other aspects of their jobs. What started out as a shared document intended for simple editing could, for example, trigger electronic brainstorming in which people quickly submit new ideas for customer outreach. Over time these shifts could become self-supporting and reduce the need for change management. The wiki tool's abilities are reflected in the organizational practices and the human skills, and vice versa.

With the idea of a mix, the fatal flaw of a silver bullet strategy is impossible. You will necessarily be taking a whole-system approach.[1] You will always be considering the tools, practices, and human aspects and looking for ways to blend them together for greater effectiveness and efficiency.

Mixing also conjures up vivid imagery that speaks to people with a variety of experiences. As I've already suggested, cooks can see ingredients being added to a pot and then mixed together to produce something far better than the individual flavors. Painters can see the different colors swirling together as paint is mixed. Chemists can see different chemicals added together in such a way as to create a whole new material—or a messy explosion if the mix isn't just right. Musicians can hear their mix. Too much bass, too little treble and mid-range, and the beauty of the composition is lost.

How do you mix in an organizational environment? How do you get from the image of mixing to an organizational reality? A good cook knows that chopped and sautéed onions, bell peppers, and celery form the base to many Cajun dishes. In organizations, it is the human capabilities, technology tools, and organizational practices that form your base. Instead of sautéing, you can negotiate the mix of your ingredients.

Negotiating a Basic Mix

Think of Stop-Look-Listen as assembling your raw ingredients. Now you have to figure out how to mix the available people, technology, and organization into something strong and valuable. Unfortunately there is no easy ratio, like the 1:2:3 for the Cajun ingredients just mentioned. However, as in cooking, there are many different ways to make a great meal. Great chefs have strong frameworks that guide them to mix wonderful, balanced flavors from new materials. Although I don't have the framework of a great culinary education, and perhaps you don't either, negotiation is something we are all familiar with. Negotiation provides the framework for you to mix compatible proportions and types of technology tools, organizational practices, and employee capabilities.

A successful negotiation is one in which the parties agree to a set of trade-offs concerning the issues of the negotiation—a set that creates as much value as possible for all the parties.[2] The basic steps to negotiating a mix are as follows:

- Identify the stakeholders.
- Make sure the stakeholders understand the value of integrative negotiation (versus a battle-style negotiation).
- Identify high-level options.
- Understand the costs and benefits.
- Problem-solve to create value for all stakeholders.

Identify Stakeholders

Brainstorm around all the people, departments, technology tools, and organizational practices that will be involved or affected by the mix. You are not going to try to juggle them all at once; rather, this initial brainstorming is the same as checking the cupboards against the recipe's list of ingredients before you begin. You want to know what you are dealing with before you start messing up the kitchen.

The cardiac care team described in Chapter Three included the surgeons, cardiac care nurses from both the night and day shifts, the rehabilitation experts, the team statistician, and others. They were smart to include the core stakeholders as well as technical support staff.

Think broadly. I say this for a couple of reasons. First, you don't want anyone to think they've been overlooked. (I'm drawing on my people savvy for this point.) Second, you want a diverse group to help you with the design. A diverse group will help you think of even more people, technology, and organizational issues that need to be considered. Pick too small a group and you're likely to overlook something. You might cover yourself by a really good listening stage, but it's better if you can include good ideas early and proactively avoid pitfalls. If these are big groups, identify who can represent the larger group's perspective, or use technology tools to gather and manage the view of a large number of participants.

Ensure Integrative Negotiation Skills

Ideally, you should either verify that the stakeholders have the basics of integrative negotiation in their skill set or provide a brief training. Integrative negotiation is more of a collaboration and joint problem-solving activity than a battle—and the distinction is important. If the stakeholders, and this includes you, don't have integrative negotiating skills, you run the risk that each stage of the negotiation will be seen as concerned with either compromise (then everybody ends up with less than what they really want) or, even worse, competition. The best dynamic for negotiation is a mixing whereby stakeholders give in on issues they don't care much about in return for getting what they want on their most important issues. The complexity in most organizational settings means that there are many issues to work with and many instances in which people want different things—enabling these trade-offs to work. Everyone may not get everything they need out of the overall mix, but all will understand why different choices were made.

Think back to the Providence cardiac care team. They didn't have an explicit negotiation focus, but recall that Dr. Brevig mentioned the importance of collaboration to their success. Also, cardiac critical care staff nurse Judy Espedal noted the value of their team's ability to take their time and focus on an issue. These organizational norms and skills support a collaborative approach to negotiating the mix of dimensions that will support the ultimate goal of a powerfully effective organization.

Identify High-Level Design Ingredients

Once you have a rough draft identifying the stakeholders and believe that at least those stakeholders most central to the process have some negotiation skills, you're ready to brainstorm about issues to be negotiated/mixed. These issues can be sorted into different categories, including the available technology tools, organizational processes, and peoples' knowledge, skills, abilities, and quirks. Consider both the possibilities and the fixed requirements that you have to incorporate into the solution. Use your list of stakeholders to help trigger possible tools, processes, and people issues to add to the mix. By this point in the identification process I generally have a spreadsheet or matrix started, with the different stakeholders listed in a row across the top and my growing list of design ingredients in a column down the left side.

Let's consider a simple example. Table 4.1 gives us the starting entries in a matrix that might go along with a decision like the one Eugene Lee faced in Chapter Two. Recall that he had to decide how to respond to his employees using the company wiki (a website that all the team members can add to and edit) to answer his (initially private) questions about their personal goals.

There are just two stakeholders noted here: Eugene (the new CEO) and the employees. In this instance the employee needs

Table 4.1. Design-Ingredient Matrix

Ingredients/Options	Stakeholders	
	New CEO	*Employees*
What to do with the employee posts already on the wiki		
What Eugene will do about his own answer to the goal question		

are likely to be similar to one another, so there is no need to consider them individually—though in real life you'd want to take a moment and make sure that's true before lumping a set of stakeholders together.

Two design ingredients come to mind:

1. What to do with the posts the employees have already made to the wiki
2. What Eugene should do about his own response to the goal question he proposed to the employees

It's not enough to think about these ingredients in general. You need to be more specific in developing a list of options. A good cookbook won't just say that you need five apples for a recipe. You need to know their weight and the variety of the apples to know the particular flavor, consistency, appropriate cooking method, and how much of the other ingredients you will need; a more sour variety of apple will need more sugar, a juicier variety may need less water. If you're building your own recipe, you may know that you want apples, but you will need to think a little bit more about the amount and type. Similarly, in a negotiation you can't speak in generalities. You need to have specific options on the table to be able to make effective trade-offs. This brings us to the next step.

Identify Different Options Within Each Ingredient

The brainstorming continues. Now the focus is on the possible options for each of the categories of ingredients. Be sure to consider the perspective of all the stakeholders as you think about the options. Not everyone has to love each of the possibilities— they are just possibilities at this stage. You could start out by thinking of options that particular stakeholders might love and options that they might hate. Also add some options that would seem to not be likely to work. I've added some possibilities to the matrix, as shown in Table 4.2.

Table 4.2. Listing Options Within Ingredients

Ingredients/Options	Stakeholders	
	New CEO	*Employees*
What to do with employee posts already on the Wiki		
Delete posted answers		
Ignore posted answers		
Comment on posted answers: start a discussion		
What Eugene will do about his own answer to the goal question		
Do nothing		
Post "company-line" type answer		
Post honest answer		

Assess Each Option's Costs and Benefits

Now we have a bunch of empty boxes. Surely something must go in those spaces. As you look at each possibility, consider how each of the stakeholders will feel about that option. I've used a rating system ranging from −10 (deal breaker; really hate it) to +10 (woo-hoo, love this outcome!) to describe how each stakeholder group might feel about each of Eugene's options, but you could use any rating scale that fits your situation. There are no rules for how the numbers work. They don't all have to be even or sum to a particular amount. The numbers are just ratings of how much you think each stakeholder will like or dislike the particular outcome.

It may be that all the stakeholders want the same thing (we call this a "congruent issue" in negotiation-speak). Think about negotiating for a job. You want the job you've been offered in the leading company in your industry. The company manager wants you to take the job. You're negotiating about the location. Location isn't the biggest issue on the table, but you would prefer to take the slot in San Francisco versus the one in Phoenix. It turns out that the company manager feels the same way. You'd both rate the San Francisco option a +4 and the Phoenix option +1. (I'm avoiding money comparisons here, because many of our mixes won't have monetary equivalents.) Everyone will be happy if you end up taking the San Francisco job.

It may be that some issues are more stereotypically a win-lose situation: You want a high salary and the manager wants to provide a lower salary. You give high salary a +8; the manager gives it −8. You give low salary −8; the manager gives it +8. You both care a lot about salary (the extreme ratings near +/−10), so the best outcome is likely to be a compromise middle salary.

I've entered some estimates using this kind of rating scale into Eugene's example matrix (see Table 4.3). The right answer is clear (if these estimates are right) and parallel what Eugene did. He chose to engage with the contributions to the wiki by adding follow-up comments to people's posts, as well as posting his own personal answer. These actions make everybody happy—a fairly straightforward solution in this case. Next, I'll add some complexity.

Many issues will be more complicated—and thus actually offer more room for collaboration. Although different stakeholder groups may want different options, they don't all care equally about the different categories overall. This is where negotiation becomes a problem-solving collaboration and very valuable for our mixing process.

Sticking with the new job scenario, think about a couple of options: the top bonus percentage you'll be eligible for and how you will move your household goods to the new location. A little background: You've been living in a studio apartment

Table 4.3. Rating the Options

Ingredients/Options	Stakeholders	
	New CEO	*Employees*
What to do with employee posts already on the wiki		
Delete posted answers	−5	−10
Ignore posted answers	0	−8
Comment on posted answers: start a discussion	+7	+10
What Eugene will do about his own answer to the goal question		
Do nothing	0	−6
Post "company-line" type answer	+3	−8
Post honest answer	+8	+10

in Chicago. You've were laid off by your last company two months ago, and your cash flow is low. The company manager prefers that you take a maximum five days of vacation and that you transport your household goods—even though you have indicated they are modest—on your own. You, not surprisingly, prefer that you have ten days vacation and that the company covers the movers and moving van.

Here's where it gets interesting. You care a lot about the moving expenses. Moving expenses are real money to you—you don't have a car or a truck and would have to either buy or rent one. You don't care so much about the vacation. Though it hasn't been a vacation, you've had a lot of free time while out of work. The manager cares a lot about the vacation time, as to give you more would be odd, given company norms. The manager doesn't care much about moving expenses, as you don't have that much to move. Table 4.4 shows the rating for each option.

Table 4.4. Rating Vacation/Moving Options

Ingredients/Options	Stakeholders	
	Job Candidate	*Hiring Manager*
Vacation Days		
Five	−2	+7
Seven	0	0
Ten	+2	−7
Moving Method		
Candidate buys a car/truck	−6	+3
Candidate rents a car/truck	−3	+3
Moving van paid for by company	+6	−3

What's the best outcome? If you settle on five days of vacation and a moving van, you get +4 "points." The manager gets +4 as well. The situation does not have to end up with an even calculation; you just need to extract the most value out of the possibilities for each of you. What trips up some less-experienced negotiators is the misguided belief that compromise—splitting the difference—generally creates a good outcome. In this case (and in many others) you would both be worse off. In a compromise, you would get −3 points and the manager would get +3. Compromising would leave you each with less than you would have (+4 for each of you) if you trade off things you care little about in exchange for things you care a lot about.

Working with More Complexity

I've used the everyday new job example as a warm-up for the complications of considering technology tools, organizational processes, and people. We've all been involved in job negotiations. We've all been involved in cooking—at the least, we've watched someone else cook—and we can now extrapolate this to recipes for plugged-in management. Through discussion, or a formal negotiation process, you can validate your initial estimates for all your stakeholders' preferences for each option. Add ingredients or break apart complex ones for greater flexibility.

I'll offer another example using a wiki. Imagine a wiki with the goal of supporting the development of proposals. Proposals require information from across the organization in terms of things like pricing, project management, time frames, and available resources. The information must be current and easily accessible. A wiki might be a simple way an organization could support the work flow.

How do you decide whether a wiki is a good idea for your company? Maybe your marketing people have already decided that it's a good idea, but now you have to figure out how to make it work.

From start to finish you need to be thinking about how you will mix together the human, technological, and organizational dimensions of design, adoption, and short- and long-term implementation. The first step is to consider the relevant stakeholders. In this instance I start with the wiki innovation lead, internal wiki contributors, external wiki contributors, and the internal information technology staff. Already this list is informed by the three dimensions. Organizational roles are relevant in terms of who will use the new approach and who will support it. The decision to allow outsiders (perhaps subcontractors) access also speaks to organizational roles and people issues. The more engaged the subcontractors are, the more likely they are to be committed to the project.[3] Blocking them from the system could hurt this engagement. The fact that a wiki is a technology tool ties to the need for explicit consideration of the information technology support staff.

The next step is to identify the high-level issues and the possible decisions to make about design and implementation. In Table 4.5 I've drafted a starter assessment of the preferences for the different stakeholders. Certainly there will be variations in terms of how individual people feel, but for this starter assessment I'm thinking of the average I'd expect for someone in that role.

The possibilities for each of the technology, organizational, and people issue or ingredient categories provide a place to start. Table 4.5 shows four design options: size of the initial membership pool, availability of support, particular editing capabilities, and how people will gain initial access to the wiki. These each cross the dimensions of people, technology tools, and organizational processes. Again, this is a starting point; discussions with the stakeholders may identify additional issues, options within issues, or even other critical stakeholders. Additionally, in the real world I might have to have several versions of this starting document, as some design decisions might preclude other choices. (A decision to focus on a patentable technology may preclude some forms of open collaboration; choosing pasta for the main course generally precludes using rice elsewhere in a menu.) It's easiest to keep those scenarios separate rather than to try to put them all on one sheet.

The size of the initial membership pool is our first opportunity to see how values can vary across the different stakeholders. The wiki lead may have the best understanding of how the number of people who have access to the wiki affects the value of the wiki.[4] The internal and external users may have some understanding of this "more the merrier" effect, but the main effect that the information technology support staff may see is that a larger group means more people to support. This assessment is then shown by the varying positive and negative ratings expected for the different stakeholder groups.

Availability of support is another area in which the information technology support staff will likely see things differently than the users do. The users are interested in higher levels of richer support, whereas the support staff will see this as an addition to their workload. For support staff already running at full capacity, this may be seen as a big cost. In such cases, adding an outcome could provide great value to all. Many organizations are looking to their customers for help in support. If a process were implemented that vetted "super users" and then provided

Table 4.5. Wiki Mix Assessment Matrix

Design Features/ Options	Stakeholders			
	Wiki Innovation Lead	*Internal Wiki Contributors*	*External Wiki Contributors*	*Internal Information Technology Staff*
Size of Initial Membership Pool				
Large	+9	+7	+7	−5
Medium	+6	+4	+4	−3
Small	+4	+2	+2	0
Support				
24/7 support available	+7	+6	+9	−9
Support available during U.S. daytime	+2	+3	+9	−4
Support only from online chat	−2	−5	−8	+5

Table 4.5. (*Continued*)

Design Features/ Options	Stakeholders			
	Wiki Innovation Lead	*Internal Wiki Contributors*	*External Wiki Contributors*	*Internal Information Technology Staff*
Editing Capabilities				
No highlighting for comments	−5	−6	−6	0
Ability to highlight areas that need additional editing	+5	+4	+3	−2
Separate discussion page to make group decisions	+3	+4	+6	−5
Type of Registration				
Verifiable registration (membership must be approved)	+3	−2	−4	+8
Referral registration allowed	+5	0	+2	−4
No registration required	+2	0	+4	−8

incentives for them to help rookie users, then all the stakeholder groups could be supported without great additional cost, and perhaps some of that cost could be borne by the marketing department.[5] That addition could be one that all the stakeholders could agree on.

One definition of a wiki is "a user-editable website." But how do the users know what edits or additions to focus on in a particular document and how to make decisions that meet the needs of the larger group? There must be some way to signal the need for additional work and a way to come to aligned decisions about what those changes should be. Highlighting and comments pages are two ways to approach these needs, and the different stakeholders may vary in terms of the value they find in the different approaches. In this example we see that the external stakeholders place greater value on the discussion page. Although a discussion page is good for the internal users, they may have alternative organizational ways to have these discussions and so be less focused on this particular technology feature. The support staff may see each feature as adding to the possibility of something breaking and needing their attention, but across all stakeholders, this issue looks to be of less overall importance.

With the last issue, things get more interesting. Skilled negotiators are always on the lookout for combinations of issues about which some stakeholders care a great deal and other stakeholders care very little. The idea is to make a trade-off and integrate the interests of the different stakeholders.[6] In this instance, if you manage the whole mix of these issues at the same time, rather than just trying to force agreement on a particular option issue by issue, you find that going with the large initial membership pool can be offset by a registration process with greater security.[7]

The best negotiators are those who plan their negotiations. The most plugged-in managers likewise plan their approaches for building new and powerful organizational strategies, structures, and practices. In both instances you are more likely to thrive to the extent that you help the other stakeholders do likewise. Think about the process as a puzzle to be solved rather than a competition to be won.

This background effort will help you position all the various stakeholders for negotiating the features and possible options within each feature. Ideally, in a mixed/collaborative negotiation, the stakeholders will trade off such that issues that are of minor importance to a group will be conceded for concessions on more important issues. For example, the information technology staff might concede that the possible security issues posed by wikis (if people can edit in a wiki, they can also delete) are acceptable as long as a verified registration process is used for logging in. The benefits of the wiki collaboration process (of major benefit to the internal wiki contributors and the wiki innovation lead) offset the security issues, given a trade-off of a more rigorous log-in process (a minor negative to the contributors, but of huge importance to the information technology staff).

OK, I'll admit it—it was hard to fill out the wiki matrix without a specific context in mind. Your own versions will be much more realistic and appropriate to your own organization because you will have a clear context to work with, just as it's easier to plan a menu for friends than one for strangers, because you start out with a basic understanding of your friends' tastes.

BUILDER

In some situations the setting may be so new to you and your organization that you have to start with a blank slate. It may be difficult even to imagine the stakeholders and options. In this case a checklist may help. You already know that you will need to consider people, technology tools, and organizational processes—but those are broad categories. This section is to help with the next level of brainstorming.

Because you're building a recipe, I've translated some of the basics of systems design into such a checklist with the acronym BUILDER.[8] As you take notes on each of these topics for your particular situation, think about how the different stakeholders might react to or view the situation differently. I offer this approach simply to help you achieve a richer level of reflection as you consider the context of your design.

Business Objectives

These are the basic motivations for what you're trying to do. You may not think of them as "business objectives," but it will certainly help you get organizational support if you do. For more personal situations, just ask: *What do I hope to gain from this new tool (say, wiki upgrade) or process (say, telecommuting)?*

Universe

What is the overall setting for this effort? Context and history are valuable both so we can learn from past efforts and to help us begin to understand the other stakeholders' interests. Understanding the interests of these stakeholders allows us to understand the motivations involved and, ideally, how to align them for design success. Have there been prior activities that make people more or less interested in supporting certain outcomes? Are there legacy technologies or policies that will color what people think?

Information Needs

Who needs what information and in what form? For example, teams generally perform better when everyone knows who knows what, who needs what information, and how to coordinate, given that knowledge.[9] Or, from a technology perspective, will colleagues need login information? Will they need basic training on how to create and edit video or how to participate effectively in discussions across time zones?

Laws

Policies, required procedures, laws, regulations, and the like are an important backdrop to any design. Perhaps you don't want these to limit your initial thinking, but ultimately they have to be considered, even if just to attempt to change them. For example, financial firms may have federal regulations regarding the archiving of communication. In those settings you must conform to regulations even in the use of social media like a wiki.

Dynamics

Dynamics include the time frame and sequencing of stakeholder interactions and the steps to build the design (for example, do I have to delete an existing application before I can install the new one?). And here's an important note: Any major information technology design should have "full backup" as a first step.

Events

By what events and milestones should the design and implementation be judged? How will you know if you are progressing in the way you hoped? What metrics can you use to track the process? Tracking is critical; without it you can't know whether you need to make adjustments.

Reach

What is the reach and magnitude of this project in terms of people, money, and number of other organizational systems touched? Reach also helps you consider the return on investment. How much investment in the process is wise or supported, given the reach?

Table 4.6 shows a completed example based on the wiki scenario to illustrate the process. These are my rough assessments for a generic organization; your own setting may be very different. The idea is to use the checklist to prepare for your more specific mixing process.

Table 4.6. Example: Use of BUILDER Checklist

In General	Example
Business objectives: Basic motivations for what you're trying to achieve.	Reduce duplication of effort. Wiki will enable a single point of reference for editing and access to information.
Universe: Context and history to learn from past efforts and to help us begin to understand the other stakeholders' interests.	Past file-sharing approach failed. Some departments felt they put in more work than others as the system was brought online.
Information needs: Who needs what information and in what form?	Everyone will need login information. Some departments will need basic training on how to create and edit videos. New hires may need information on how to participate effectively in 24/7 work cycles.
Laws: Policies, required procedures, regulations, and the like are an important backdrop to any design.	Legal team will need to assess whether company's document retention strategy makes sense with a wiki.
Dynamics: The time frame and sequencing of stakeholder interactions.	Back up information on the current file-sharing system (any major information technology design should have "full backup" as a first step). Seed some of the wiki pages with key information to provide value from the first day. "Go live" day should follow a holiday and not be near the close of a fiscal quarter.

Table 4.6. (*Continued*)

In General	Example
Events: By what milestones should the design and implementation be judged?	Gather data from the last employee survey about how much time they spent looking for information. Check with the marketing department on the length of time and related overtime for last year's response to requests for proposals. Save this data and compare the following implementation of the wiki.
Reach: What is the magnitude of this project in terms of people, money, and number of other systems touched? Reach also helps us consider the ROI. How much investment in the process is wise or supported, given the reach?	The wiki will cross all functional areas of the organization and will require a period of extra development and support from the information technology department. Budget issues should be sorted out in advance of final adoption decision.

Can something you're trying to mix really fit in a bunch of boxes guided by an acronym?

Probably not. Our technologies, organizational processes, and knowledge, skills, abilities, and quirks are all evolving. That said, these boxes and checklists help you keep your various ingredients in order. Professional cooks call this *mise en place* ("everything in place"; that is, assembling all the ingredients and utensils you'll need to follow a recipe before you begin).[10] Without some kind of organizing structure, you could easily end up with a terrible mess.

You can use your organizing structure (the draft matrix) as your base recipe. Work with your stakeholders to improve on the base and keep it up to date. This collaborative, negotiated approach is likely to result in a final outcome that is different—better overall—from the outcome imagined by any one party at the outset. By collaborating and intelligently mixing, a better outcome can often be achieved in a way that meets more of the needs of each of the stakeholders. Solutions that meet more stakeholder needs are a solid foundation for design and implementation success. It's in everyone's best interest to work with the mix you've developed if their needs are being met.

To conclude this chapter, here are two examples; one an example of what happens when you start with consideration of your stakeholders and mix according to their needs, the other an example of what happens when you do not.

Southwest Airlines Makes a Change

Few people these days go to the airport expecting to fully understand what will happen from arrival to departure. Airport changes of any type can result in anger and delays if the changes take passengers by surprise. You may recall the early weeks of the "3–1–1" practice in U.S. airports: three-ounce container, one-quart clear plastic bag, one bag per passenger.

I experienced the exception that proves the "airport change equals anger" rule on Southwest Flight 2001 from San Jose to Los Angeles. About three years earlier, Southwest changed its boarding policy from A/B/C groups (first to stand in line, first on the plane) to sequentially numbered boarding passes (based on when you check in) and numbered signage in the boarding areas indicating, in clusters of five, where to stand once boarding was announced. Under the new system, you don't need to be standing in line until just a few minutes before boarding.

Any change of this magnitude takes a while to be understood and accepted by customers, especially when you fly over a hundred million passengers a year and the change touches each one of those passengers. When Southwest first implemented the boarding line change, I noticed some bewildered passengers: some not sure where to stand, others double checking that their fellow line standers were in exact order, people asking if they had to sit in seat A21 (mistaking their check-in number with a seat assignment), and people just unhappy with the greater number of signs in the waiting area.

Although there were some growing pains, Southwest clearly showed its plugged-in management expertise in the implementation of this new procedure. From a review of the new system: "Regardless of the wrinkles, the new boarding procedure is far superior to the old. Perhaps even more important is that Southwest has demonstrated that it listens to its customers."[11]

Changing the boarding process entailed a complex adjustment. Not only did Southwest have to revamp internal and public-facing technologies (for example, the online check-in system and the kiosk check-in systems at the airport), but they also had to train their personnel and develop user-friendly information and signage that their diverse passengers could easily understand (from families with kids who travel rarely, to people who travel every week). Their customer complaint ratio remains the lowest of any major U.S. airline,[12] and I, for one, think the new boarding process feels less like a cattle call. Had Southwest focused only on the software or its employees and not done what they could to help passengers make sense of the whole experience, the result might have been a nightmare for both the company and the passengers.

How Mixing Can Support, or Ensnare, Your Customers

Contrast the Southwest transition with the experience of learning to use point of sale (POS) terminals to swipe your credit or debit card to pay for your purchases at a checkout stand. Although the glitches we encounter at an automated checkout stand are much less traumatic than not getting the seat you want on a three-hour airplane ride, they are a useful contrast to the Southwest experience, given their similar customer-facing nature.

I'll use a major grocery store chain as an example, though I've seen the same story play out in other retail settings. This grocery chain implemented customer POS terminals around the same time that other chains did. The POS terminal sits on the little counter we used to use just to write our checks. The POS terminals are physically obvious, so they are likely to trigger customer understanding of their use.[13] Customers have come to understand that they do not have to hand their credit or debit cards to the checkout person (a shift made for security) to be swiped. The customer experience beyond this point, however, is not standard. Some systems require that the card be swiped early in the checkout process, others don't accept the swipe until after all the items are entered; some systems have the "Accept" button on the lower right, others on the lower left; and so on. These variations are the result of software and customer-interface differences.

The particular grocery store chain I have in mind recently "upgraded" their POS customer interface. The customer interface change is all software and so is less likely to trigger customer understanding than would a physical change. There was no effort to support the customers through the change (most obviously, letting them know that they must now wait to swipe until all items have been entered—which, interestingly, seems to increase total time in line). I observed multiple people making multiple swipes before asking the checkout person for help (yes, I did it too). As a result, the checkout people have created handwritten signs with instructions and taped these signs to the POS terminals. Kudos to the frontline people for adjusting the recipe to support the people aspect of the change.

The grocery store management apparently thought only about their technology ingredients and not the whole recipe. The grocery had a technical reason to change the software, so they made that technical change. Management did not make any organizational process changes (they could have asked the checkout people to include a comment about the change, in the same way they ask "Did you find everything you needed today?"). Management does not seem to have considered the customers' perceptions or use of the POS terminal. The checkout people, on the other hand, were clearly plugged in. They saw the new technology, they observed the trouble customers had with the change, and they created a new practice (attach a small explanatory sign) to help with customer understanding.

Certainly the Southwest and POS examples vary in many regards. Boarding practices are a major customer experience issue for flying, whereas POS terminals are probably less important to the overall retail experience. Southwest's customers may fly rarely and so perhaps are more attentive to instructions, whereas retail customers deal with a variety of POS systems often and so may assume they understand the routine. Many of Southwest's customers use the web interface and so have access to additional information about the boarding process change— not a reasonable expectation for a grocery chain. Do these differences mean it is more or less important for Southwest to plug in and mix together people, technology, and organizational ingredients in a whole-system way? Perhaps there is a higher value proposition for Southwest; but the low cost to the grocery means, in my estimation, that the grocery would also have had a positive return on its investment—had they done more than think about the technology ingredient alone.

Southwest's successful mix is exemplary in terms of using all three kinds of ingredients and is an effective, if abstract, negotiated approach to manage a complex process. (I don't believe they formally called this a negotiation.) They took the range of stakeholders into account and adjusted human, technical, and organizational ingredients into a well-balanced system that succeeded. I also expect that they are tracking customer comments and boarding speed to determine whether the recipe needs further adjustments.

Southwest's case shows that for the plugged-in manager, mixing means addressing technology, organizational process, and human understanding all at once, in an integrated way. It isn't enough for the implementers of change to enjoy the outcome—the implementers must support how all the stakeholders will be affected. This can take place through a formal declared negotiated process, or one that proceeds as if a negotiation were taking place—a more tacit approach. As long as stakeholder needs are explicitly considered, the design outcomes should mimic a formal negotiation. There may, however, be less commitment, given that the other stakeholders were not formally involved in the process (they may see it as "not invented here"); there is less initial understanding (they haven't been working on the design and so will have to learn how it works); and there is less creativity in the design, given that a less diverse set of stakeholders was involved in any brainstorming.

Next Steps

We've explored mixing, the second practice of the plugged-in manager. The third practice is how to help others get plugged in by sharing your own plugged-in methods. In the next chapter I show how managers share their ability to mix and by doing so create more powerful and effective organizations.

chapter
FIVE

Third Practice: Sharing

You've identified key stakeholders. You've created a list of ingredients and options. You've negotiated a mix of technology tools, organizational practices, and human capabilities and needs. Now that you have a base recipe, how do you bring others along so that they can share in the hard work?

Sharing is the third practice of the plugged-in manager.

If you don't share, then every action you take toward getting plugged in is a full-blown implementation effort—in terms of both having to explain yourself for every move and having the motivation to work in a plugged-in way. You're either on the bus or off the bus. If you are committed to the plugged-in approach, you have to share the ideas with your colleagues.

Sharing means that others understand your plugged-in approach and can work in parallel. In a well-organized kitchen, too many cooks do not spoil the broth. On the contrary, they share the workload, help innovate with new flavors, and through their own diverse needs help create ways of working that will benefit a wider variety of people.

Zappos shows the value of sharing in how it has found a way to help others develop culture savvy. Culture savvy, like plugged-in expertise, is a complex area of organizational proficiency that is often learned by experience and challenge, not just by reading or hearing a lecture.[1] Zappos offers both organizational outsiders and insiders a way to learn their approach to company culture through a variety of rich experiences and dialogue.[2] Two of their websites serve as examples:

- ZapposInsights.com. A website and community about what makes Zappos unique and how Zappos does business. They offer free open tours and formal management training and even have a section on the site called "Ask Anything." (The story in the introduction to Part Two about the Zappos warehouse design started out as an "Ask Anything" question I submitted.)
- DeliveringHappinessBook.com. A website and web community about the ideas in Zappos CEO Tony Hsieh's book *Delivering Happiness*, which gives advice for start-ups. Zappos is sharing, so they want us to share too: "Our higher purpose? Delivering happiness to the world. Make it yours too and help spread the word to family, friends and colleagues alike!"

I believe that rich experiences are at the heart of helping others learn any complex systems skills. Need additional evidence? Consider leadership and design.

Leadership savvy is another complex area that is best taught through modeling, learning by doing, and reflection. In the fourth edition of their best-selling book *The Leadership Challenge*, Jim Kouzes and Barry Posner write that leadership, like any skill, "can be strengthened, honed, and enhanced, given the motivation and desire, along with practice and feedback, role models, and coaching."[3] In the related instructors' guide, they continue:

"In our own studies, as well as others by the Center for Creative Leadership and corporations like Honeywell, three major opportunities for learning to lead emerge: (a) trial and error, (b) observation of others, and (c) formal education and training" (pp. ix–x).[4]

Similarly, Dan Saffer, writing for the Adaptive Path blog, says:

> I was taught [at Carnegie Mellon's School of Design] that design has three components: thinking, making, and doing. (Doing is the synthesis, presentation, and evaluation of a design; the bridge between thinking and making.)
>
> Details often get overlooked in just "thinking" projects, as do constraints. Constraints are somehow less solid in the world of thought than they are in the world of making.[5]

So how do we help others become plugged in? By using the same ideas that Zappos, Kouzes, Posner, and Saffer offer for spreading other complex skills: provide opportunities to try (and perhaps fail) to observe others and to get formal training when it's appropriate. We all have to get our hands dirty if we're going to do this well.

In the examples that follow, you'll see that modeling plugged-in management and giving colleagues the chance to try plugged-in approaches on their own are the running themes. In none of the examples does a leader say "Be plugged in—do this . . ." Instead, these leaders shine a spotlight on plugged-in management through alignment with work that needs to get done, opportunities for others to develop their own plugged-in methods in challenging situations, focusing on high-profile lead-user examples, and "thinking out loud" as they further develop their own plugged-in practices. And besides, sometimes it's just more fun in a group.

I'll close the chapter by talking about how to choose a particular approach. Formal and informal learning both have their place, and plugged-in managers know how to choose between the two and how to mix them together.

Don't Let the Words Get in Your Way

Stewart Mader helps organizations build wikis into their workflow. (Recall that wikis are websites that are editable by their users and readers.) They can be as open as allowing anyone to edit (such as Wikipedia), open to only a particular project group, and everything in between. Stewart has been at this for as long as wikis have been possible and is currently director, social and online tools, at the CFA Institute.

Stewart's book *Wikipatterns* focuses on project and community practices that happen to use a wiki.[6] His approach incorporates a clear understanding of the variety of expertise and attitudes brought to each wiki project. His plugged-in management skill is evident in how he blends these different dimensions of each project.

In a long conversation one rainy day in San Francisco, Stewart shared a valuable insight into helping organizations rework their work using technology when it's beneficial: Don't let the words get in your way.[7] That is, don't let the terms (for example, wiki, open innovation, Enterprise 2.0) put a barrier between you and the people you're helping to understand the plugged-in way. Focus on the work.

Stewart gives an example in his book, in which he talks of project and community support that happens to use a wiki. He follows his own advice in thinking about how technology tools and meeting practice might work together:

> Instead of emailing the agenda, put it on a wiki page and email people a link to that page. If changes need to be made, anyone can do so and everyone will have immediate access to the same, up-to-date version. Then, record minutes on the wiki so all information pertinent to the

meeting is in one place. The further advantage here is that
the responsibility to take minutes doesn't have to rest with
just one person. No matter how carefully one person listens
and takes notes, it's really difficult for one person to accurately
capture everything that happens during the course of a
meeting. One person may pick up on a certain detail that
another person misses, so using the wiki can give everyone
a place to contribute, resulting in a more comprehensive
account of the meeting.

Keeping meeting agendas and minutes on the wiki can be
the perfect foundation for project and task management. As
various topics and items from a meeting are discussed and
need further action, new wikipages can spawn from the
agenda or minutes and be used to manage them.[8]

His description isn't about a specific technology or philoso-
phy; rather, it's about getting the work done. He describes how
to integrate the technology and the organizational practice, but
the focus is on the work outcomes rather than the trendiness of
the approach or talking through the differences between a wiki
or a blog (blogs tend to be more like a newspaper column with a
single or small number of authors, whereas a wiki can be any kind
of webpage).

In our meeting, Stewart highlighted the importance of
helping people realize that, technology or not, they're interde-
pendent with others in today's organizations. If the people in the
organization don't think about this interconnectedness, then
they're less likely to collaborate, add to a wiki, or even provide an
agenda. It is hard to see the value of that kind of effort without
understanding the underlying interdependence of their work
with that of their colleagues.

I asked him about how he talks about Enterprise 2.0 or E2.0
(a broad and much-debated term used to describe how some
companies use emergent collaboration and work practices, like
wikis and Facebook, to support their business). He noted that

people can spend too much time debating what the terms should be. More specifically:

> People are so caught up in ideological arguments around what it should be called. All are weak. When I go into an organization, I help them find the best content that people write internally and then amplify that using their social media. I help people structure their job responsibilities, line them up to their personal goals—measured the same way as any other job. Making sure the internal organization is properly equipped in terms of [technology tools, organizational process, people skills] to support that work—it doesn't need a term applied to it because it's part and parcel of their work. Makes it as efficient as possible.
>
> What I find useless about the whole [Enterprise 2.0 terminology] discussion is that when you create a new term for something, you create a distinction that makes the casual observer think it's totally different. For example: blogger versus journalist . . . There are some variations in research, ethics, pay, but functionally they're the same. When people get caught up in the terminology, they lose focus on the part that's the same . . .
>
> Slows down implementation as they think it's about adoption. But in reality in an organization, you want people to get work done, first and foremost. If you create a divide, Enterprise 1.0, 1.5 . . . you have people thinking that they need to do additional work to drive adoption of each "new" thing. This creates a false conflict between "management mandate" and "grassroots effort," when in reality all you need to do is find the best examples of strong, coordinated teamwork and help them become standards throughout the organization.

Experts often use jargon to signal their expertise. That is a great way to set yourself apart—but is that your goal when you are trying to share plugged-in approaches? That's not what I heard in my conversation with Stewart. When I asked Stewart about the word he uses when he first talks to a group about a consulting engagement, he produced a vivid image:

> "Barn raising" is often the first term I use to describe a session designed to help a group structure their collaborative efforts. It sounds nothing like a technology jargon term because it originated in farming communities in the mid-1800s. People would get together to pool efforts and build each farmer's barn in time for the harvest. By [people] working together, barns were constructed in less time, and the best construction techniques made their way into more structures than if people worked individually.

It is not about the words, it is about the work. Help people see the value of plugging in from the perspective of their work. Do not lose the part that is "the same" while demonstrating the part that is different.

Nucor: Hire the Right People, Then Let Them Learn

Nucor is the largest producer of steel in the United States and the world's foremost steel recycler. They are also a great example of transparency at work, the value of team-based pay, and lean management. Dan Krug, director of human resources at Nucor, made clear in an interview with me that Nucor starts with the recruiting process in terms of thinking about people as well as technology and organizational practice. He said, "We are good at assessing people: Whether you're twenty-two or sixty-two, [we assess] in terms of the level of responsibility you'll own, whether you trust people, and what you think is possible."[9] Nucor-style transparency also begins during recruiting. In their on-campus interviews for new college grads, they work hard to communicate the expectations. They also bring people into the plants. "Line leaders do the recruiting and tell them how it is," Dan said. Then the offers are "not leadership development jobs, but real jobs."

Nucor, like many companies with deep plugged-in roots, believes in learning by doing. "The classroom is not a good place to learn about how Nucor operates," Dan told me. He said that safety and technology basics are taught in the classroom before the new hires suit up, but then, "After a week or two, the team is responsible for helping you learn. [The] best learning is on the shop floor. The team has a vested interest."

What the new hires are doing in those first weeks is learning from their teammates. "They see how they tackle issues . . . what happens when they fail," Dan says. "Until they see it and watch it happen, it's hard to participate in the culture."

When I asked Doyle Hopper, general manager of Nucor's Vulcraft plant (which is featured in Chapter Seven), if he was surprised by how things worked at Nucor, he related the company's culture to his personal experience: "Honestly, no. I grew up on a farm . . . family business. Family was high on work ethic. If you don't work, you don't play. Nobody's going to do it for you. Don't expect people to owe you. If you want to be better, figure out a way."

When Doyle decided farming wasn't the road he wanted to take, he interviewed with Nucor. In 1993 Nucor/Yamata offered him the "lowest position you could have," he said. "Nucor took a chance. I was fortunate to work for some great people who had the same work ethic and values." He continued, "That's the thing about Nucor, it's all team driven. If you're not pulling your weight people will let you know. One person's lack of hard work can hurt the whole team."

Doyle suggests that people dig in and learn from those with the experience: "Find the network that is successful in the area where you're not." Maintenance was his background, and though he wasn't an electrician, he ran a successful maintenance program with a lot of electrical components. He didn't know a lot but knew people who did. "That's what Nucor is teaching. You don't have to be an expert, but you do have to be driving towards learning and improvement . . . with humility. Don't let pride stand in the way of your success." In other words, plugged-in managers drive toward learning and improvement—across all of technology, organizational process, and people——wherever others have experience and they do not.

Learning by doing, and learning by doing across a range of work, forces you to confront the need to develop plugged-in management skill—even if you aren't calling it that. The work itself will highlight the missing links if you aren't considering the whole system: the people, technology, and organization dimensions. Nucor allows people to learn by doing and understands that there will be failures. Doyle gave me the short version of how to succeed: "Hire the right people. Trust them. Empower. If they mess up, you don't kill them; learn and go on."

Get in Tune

Be aware of different perceptions of technology tools, organizational practice, and skills. Even if you keep the focus on the work as you share plugged-in approaches, realize that your personal perception of the work may be different from that of your colleagues. Technology backgrounds vary. Work experiences vary. Work arrangements can vary. Different perceptions may be more or less accurate than your own—or just different. It doesn't really matter. What does matter is that you are aware of the differences and help to find ways to integrate the different views into any changes you hope to make.

A good example is Ben Kepes, the principal and founder of Diversity Analysis, a consulting company helping companies think about their business strategies, especially around how "cloud computing" may play a changing role in those strategies.[10] Based in New Zealand, he works as an industry analyst, consultant, and journalist.

I had seen Ben's *Change the System, Not the Technology* blog post and knew immediately that he understood plugged-in management. He ended the post (describing a couple of communication faux pas he had experienced) with this:

> But all of this isn't merely an exasperated rant—rather it's a cry to think about culture, not technology. All the micro-blogging, collaboration, e-this, i-that and mobile everything else technology in the world is of little effect if the people within the organization have a culture that doesn't encourage responsiveness, dialogue and open-communications. So please, people—focus on the system, not the technology. . . ."

I wondered how he applied his plugged-in skills in his consulting and management. In our interview we talked about how people in different roles may have very different expertise in plugging in and the impact these differences can have in the organization.[12]

Talking about his experience mixing people, technology, and organization in different settings, Ben raised the common problem of an organization trying to implement "some whizbang technology, but either [the technology] doesn't work [as expected], or the culture doesn't accept it." We've all seen this silver bullet approach and know it doesn't work.

How could the situation be improved? Ben gave me an example that made a lightbulb go off:

> One of my businesses is a manufacturing company. White-collar and blue-collar. Slowly [white-collar management has] been implementing some collaboration technology. Really simple tools: email, calendar, manufacturing planning. It's interesting to watch our [blue-collar] facility managers grasp the stuff. The technology doesn't work the way they think.

Ben's comment might seem to be saying that the technology doesn't work the way the blue-collar folks *think it works*. In fact, what Ben was actually saying is that the particular technology doesn't work the way the blue-collar folks in his company *think*! The mental models held by people in the blue-collar roles are different from those held by people in the white-collar roles. One is not better or more sophisticated than the other—but they are different.

> White-collar [management] deploys a tool that they [believe] is entirely obvious. Unfortunately that's not the way it works for the [blue-collar] workers. Difficulty [for the people supporting the implementation] is there is a balancing act. To a certain extent the blue-collar folks need to use the tools, but you have to balance between requiring them to use [them] and the underlying cultural aspects.

If the implementation support team didn't understand this balancing act, Ben said, there would be a "huge disconnect, blue-collar workers would feel alienated; people deploying the tools, really concerned." Ben noted that the problems could spread throughout the organization and even disenfranchise the people making the purchasing decisions as they see the investment causing conflict.

Ben suggests two solutions:

- Use focus groups to talk about what technology and practice changes might work—though groupthink could be a problem if the focus groups give the answers that they think you want to hear.
- Better: Build transorganizational groups from many different departments from the beginning. Clarify with focused messages. For example, open with: "We need some ideas about the problem we're trying to solve. We're trying to ensure that communication and collaboration can happen across disparate geographical teams." The idea is to

get everyone (or at least representatives from the different groups) together in a room and let them work toward the goal. Have the approach be focused on the goals, rather than on the tools. (*Focus on the work*—sound familiar?)

The second solution highlights an understanding that the members of the different departments and organizational roles (blue-collar and white-collar) will have different ways of understanding the technology tools and organizational practices in play. How these groups think differs by their context and goals. By working together on the task, the teams can learn who knows what, who needs to know what, and how to coordinate in the given setting with the given tools. Experts on managing teams in organizations would call this a great way of developing transactive memory, a valuable team capability.[13]

The different roles have different types of experience and skills, different ways of thinking, that lead them to these different perspectives. Their practical understanding, their wisdom, is set in different contexts. Even if they all have a whole-systems sense of the connections between technology and organizational practice, their plugged-in approach will be set in their own unique context. Only by working together to create a common context, as Ben suggests in the transorganizational group approach, can they gain value from their diverse perspectives and build a system of technology tools and organizational practices that adds value for all.

Shine a Light on Plugged-In Activities

Sometimes you don't have to manage a whole-system change from start to finish, but rather just find people in the organization who are already doing the things that plugged-in management would suggest. For example, Megan Gailey's job is all about helping people be effective at work. She is executive director of sales development at Maxim Integrated Products and has worked for tech leaders Xilinx, National Semiconductor, and Cisco. In her past and current roles she helps her communities learn to mix their available technology tools and organizational practices with an understanding of the skills and needs of the people involved. Megan is a plugged-in leader and helps others develop this capability as she promotes change in the organization.

Her approach uses demonstration and evidence to bring technology and practice solutions into the workplace. For example, she recalls joining an organization that, though global, seemed to be overlooking the value that collaboration technologies could provide for team meetings and support. Megan took a whole-systems approach to the situation: She reached out to her network of technical experts for advice on the different technical options, given the company's needs and workflow; she worked with corporate IT to consider the technical environment; and then she looked for the early adopters and situations where there would be strong value—in this case, getting a far-flung set of experts into virtual meetings to pass along their knowledge and to save this knowledge for future use.

Megan explained:

> I tend to focus on the people who are the willing participants . . . the early adopters. Through their demonstration and behavior change . . . [they] show success. [The success] sways the resistors and the people on the fence. Get the earlier adopters excited and the fence people come along.
>
> I think that helps in the tech environment. The engineers need demonstrated evidence to accept and adopt. You have to show them a case, a pilot, a success, and then you can persuade.

A strength of Megan's demonstration approach is that it helps people see the situation in context—as a part of an overall system.

It is from intertwining organizational practices, technology features, and implementation that you create new ways of working. The same level of value can't be generated from stand-alone technologies or organizational adjustments. Megan's engineers seem to have an innate understanding of this and want to make their judgment based on the combination of effects. Megan has found a strategy that shows the full system at work in the given setting and with peers doing the demo—very powerful!

Each of the preceding stories shows the value of helping others develop plugged-in management through hands-on effort. That's the way most of us learned it, and it turns out to be a fine way to help others in their own development. The next example also supports a hands-on approach, though in this instance we see the value of sharing some basic ideas first.

Teach Some Basics, Then Get Out of the Way

Jennifer Kenny, CEO of BizTH!NK, is a geologist by training. She notes that geology is systems thinking at its most fundamental. She's spent the last twenty-five years integrating technology and business and this systems background has been critical to her success.[14] I asked how she would help others understand and practice systems thinking; specifically, "How do you help them become plugged-in managers—managers able to weave technology, organizations, and people together for effective solutions?" Jennifer made it very clear that people don't learn plugged-in management via training alone. Training is typically about information that people are supposed to learn—as a trainer you know some information, and the other people are supposed to learn it. Jennifer believes that systems thinking is better demonstrated through helping people "mobilize their own ideas."

Jennifer gave this example of how you would do this in a real work situation:

A friend of mine took a new job managing a several-hundred-person loan processing support group at a bank. Things weren't going well with the how the work flowed from one area to the next, and the group was working to implement a multimillion-dollar workflow technology to solve the problem. The project was having a rough time, and my friend was frustrated with their progress. She asked my team to bring in their consulting expertise.

I asked, "What would happen if the people were involved?" Given my friend wasn't happy with the current work the loan processing group was doing, she wasn't sure that participation would have much to offer to the workflow change—but I said my team could give it a shot. The bank support group put a hold on the technology implementation work and instead looked at human coordination. About 10 percent of the group was asked (and agreed) to attend workshops on how to design their own processes.

Note that these were workshops about taking different perspectives (loan processors', salespeople's) and learning a new process (how do you learn about the different organizational roles and the related performance goals that people in the different roles work with?). This was not training focused on learning facts, information, or details that someone else had prepared.

Jennifer continued:

Next step was for the full group to meet with the senior VP of the group and my team. The SVP was clear: Unanimous support was needed to move ahead, or the consultants would be out and they'd go back to the earlier approach.

Did the subgroup that went through the workshops really believe in the new approach? Was the subgroup able to convey the same enthusiasm to the full group of several hundred? The result, Jennifer reported, was unanimous approval.

The participative approach was rolled out to the full group and later on to three other groups. They kept the hold on the big technology project and ended up with a minor modification to the technology tools they already had. As a bonus, Jennifer said, "Three hundred and fifty people came back to us and said 'I'm enjoying work I've always hated before.'"

Helping this group practice plugged-in management wasn't about training. Jennifer says these workshops were "joint design sessions."

> We knew that they knew a thousand times more about their actual work than we did—training wouldn't make sense. Instead, we helped them tap into their knowledge using the common language about their work—mobilization of their own ideas. Joint design, metrics, and analysis. Collaboration and co-invention is what's going on. We were precipitating versus leading . . . Doing systems work is being able to listen. Deep listening.

Deep listening was being demonstrated and supported. Jennifer's team showed that the way that they'd been trained to do the work was "input-process-output." "They had no understanding of the bigger game they were playing in," she said, "and that was why the handoffs were problematic: no context."

For example, the loan processing group hadn't understood that the people in the sales part of the business had quotas to meet. Only by listening did this part of the context become clear.

> We also brought the sales folks into design with them. Until then sales had been the people who screamed when they didn't get what they wanted. Next was to show all of them working across an entire system, rather than each person as a single cog. Then they saw context upon context and why it all connected. Once people begin to get context, they start looking for it themselves. Gave them the bigger picture.

The results speak for themselves (as measured by the bank's own customer satisfaction team):

- A 13 percent increase in customer satisfaction in a three-month period
- A 4 percent increase in responsiveness
- A 10 percent improvement in quality of service for performance in documentation, credit, and collateral

Jennifer's story illustrates that formal training can give people only background and context foundations on which to build their own plugged-in management expertise. Other support can then come from suggesting new ways of seeing their own role, the situations of the people around them, how the policies and practices of their organization link to their role and those of others, and how technology can be mixed in—or not.

There is another benefit to guiding rather than "training" people toward plugging in: As people begin their plugged-in practice—I'm using the term as you would for "medical practice" or "law practice"—others can see and react. As noted earlier, demonstrations from early adopters are helpful, group efforts are helpful, and in the next case, being explicit is helpful in that it helps people coordinate their practice with others'.

Don't Hide Your Plugged-In Practice

It's great if you are plugged-in. It's even better if you practice it in public. This is actually good advice for all whole-systems management, not just situations where technology is playing a role.

As Nilofer Merchant says in her organizational strategy book, *The New How*:

> If, say, only a small group of leaders knows why decisions are being made the way they are, it leaves the rest of the organization in the dark. It suggests to people that there's

some "all-powerful wizard" behind the mysterious curtain who is the only one with the ability to make things happen, and that each of us is not a co-creator. It can leave the organizational players believing they have no say in what is being decided.[15]

From Nilofer's perspective, you not only gain improved coordination from being explicit about your plugged-in practice, but you also gain motivation and commitment.

Plugging in starts with the ability to see and understand the possibilities of all the human, technical, and organizational options available to you. Plugged-in managers either don't have, or can overcome, a bias toward stand-alone technical or organizational solutions. Instead, plugged-in managers look at how they can build whole systems out of combinations of people, technical tools, and organizational processes. But here's the problem: If you practice plugged-in management in private, your good decisions have less power.

Explicit plugged-in practice means that you help others clearly see that you are considering your people, technology, and organizational options and are working to mix them together for the best organizational effect. Explicit use of plugged-in practice is better than tacit use in that others can learn from your example—as people do from Rhonda Winter's practice of thinking out loud.

I learned about Rhonda when I saw a story about her becoming the first CIO of the Indianapolis Motor Speedway (Indy 500, Brickyard 400). The article covered her management background, highlighting her experience in building teams from scratch, including a new information technology group for the National Collegiate Athletic Association (NCAA). In that story she said, "The key to a good mentor is one who reveals thinking process— someone who thinks out loud" and "Thinking out loud goes both ways . . ."[16] When we spoke, she noted that the mentoring relationship is illuminating for both parties; her mentees often teach her in turn by reacting to her positions from new perspectives.[17]

I asked Rhonda how she came to see the value of thinking out loud. Her answer showed a plugged-in management mind-set from the earliest days of her career:

> I was managing by the time I was twenty-six. Most other folks were older and more traditional. If you say, "Can you think out loud with me?" then even the most bashful will enter the conversation. We may not make the decisions that day, but we get the conversation started.
>
> [Thinking out loud is a] great teaching tool, it helps make clear that it's OK to make a mistake—it creates an environment where you can play with the ideas out loud; the first idea may not be best, but it's the conversation starter.

Thinking out loud is a great way to model plugged-in management. Getting others to think out loud adds even more value, as the group can learn during the process.

Explicit, public use of plugged-in management approaches like thinking out loud is better than tacit, private use because public and explicit use also allows others to coordinate. Think about the benefits gained in a project kickoff meeting if the group comes to a set of explicit decisions about where files will be stored, how sign-offs will be managed, and the best strategies for communicating.

Coordination can also be more physical. I had a recent phone call with a building supply vendor who carefully laid out the options for transporting and off-loading some recycled plastic panels: Would a forklift be available to lift the pallet off the truck? If not, would at least one person be available to join with the driver in off-loading by hand? Both scenarios illustrate the value of working together to make technology and practice trade-offs.

Plugged-in managers don't want to hide their plugged-in practice. They don't want other people to hide their plugged-in practice either.

How Can I Help Others Plug In?

You can help others get plugged in by thinking back to the practices highlighted by the plugged-in managers in this chapter and putting them into action in your workplace:

- Don't let the words get in your way: A particular vocabulary is less important than the work itself.
- Be aware of different perceptions of technology tools, organizational process, and skills: Frustrations arise over differences in understanding rather than the ideas themselves.
- Shine a light on plugged-in activities where you find them. Someone, somewhere in your organization is already practicing plugged-in management; highlight their efforts and take advantage of their credibility.
- Teach some basics, then let the people closest to the work design the system.
- Don't hide your plugged-in practice: Being public with your practice can aide coordination and motivation.
- Think out loud: This adds an explanatory layer to our plugged-in practice that can help others understand how and what we're doing. Getting others to think out loud with us creates a richer context for how best for the group to weave the technology, organization, and people dimensions together.

What About a Formal Training Program?

The issue is determining when more formal or less formal learning approaches are valuable. Except for our discussions of the foundations training in Jennifer Kenny's example and, earlier, the parallels between leadership savvy and plugged-in management skills, we haven't been talking here about formal training. Instead, the focus has been on hands-on and other informal strategies for plugged-in management development. There is some value to formal learning strategies for plugged-in management skills; I certainly try to convey some basic frameworks to my students before they turn on their laptops and start learning on their own (or maybe they're just checking Facebook; I'm not always sure . . .).

First, here is a comparison of informal and formal learning from Jay Cross's 2006 book *Informal Learning*:

> Formal and informal learning are ranges along a continuum of learning. Formal learning is accomplished in school, courses, classrooms, and workshops. It's official, it's usually scheduled, and it teaches a curriculum. . . .
>
> Informal learning often flies under the official radar. It can happen intentionally or inadvertently. . . . No one assigns grades, for success in life and work is the measure of its effectiveness. No one graduates, because learning never ends. . . . Examples are learning through observing, trial-and-error, calling the help line, asking a neighbor. . . .[18]

To which I would add: or searching on the Internet.[19]

Jay and I have had formal and informal opportunities to discuss different ways of learning, and I knew his work would help me focus my own ideas.[20] In his book's opening, Jay asks, "Why is this topic important?" and provides his own response: "Workers learn more in the coffee room than in the classroom. They discover how to do their jobs through informal learning: talking, observing others, trial and error, and simply working with people in the know."[21]

Jay spends much of his own time engaged in informal learning and is considered an informal learning guru. He travels the world talking to managers, technology vendors, consultants,

Figure 5.1 Value of Formal and Informal Learning

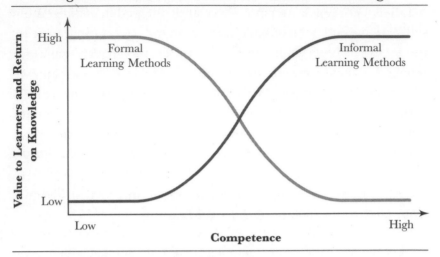

Source: Adapted from Cocheu & Griffith (2008).

and researchers who support informal learning within and across all kinds of organizations. Yet even he will acknowledge that what we are after is "the best mix of formal and informal means."[22]

Ted Cocheu is the founder and CEO of Altus, the leading provider of on-demand video management applications (an important approach for both formal and informal learning in organizations). He and I took on the issue of the best mix of formal and informal learning as we were working with a global Fortune 100 science/technology company. We developed Figure 5.1 to illustrate that, depending on the learner's current competence, formal and informal learning have different values.[23]

Think about the last time you had to sit through a formal class session on a topic in which you already had a good background. Now add the limitation that you don't have access to your PDA or an open internet connection. You probably (1) were bored, (2) asked questions that were ahead of the rest of the class—possibly disrupting the flow, and (3) spent a lot of time thinking about what a waste of time this was for you. If you'd had an internet connection, you could have been quietly digging deeper into the material and then, during the break, asked the presenter some key questions—all actions that qualify as informal learning, albeit in a classroom setting.

Formal training can have value as people begin to develop their plugged-in management approach. Novices need a structure or scaffold on which to build their base knowledge, and formal learning approaches are ideal for this. Formal training efforts should focus on the basic framework of a whole-system mix of technology tools, organizational process, and an understanding of the people involved, animated by the Stop-Look-Listen practice. Hook them with one of the vivid examples in this book or from your own experience, and then reel them in with a clear-cut framework and set of next steps. Consider whether a negotiation class would provide a running start for learning to work with other stakeholders.

As your team's expertise grows, value is more likely found in the methods of informal learning. Offer Chapter Four as background (if you haven't gifted each team member with the whole book!), and then try these steps:

- Help team members find personal ways to expand their experience.
- See how your organization's budget or other formal practices support plugged-in approaches. In cases where these formal practices don't support plugged-in management, use the situation as a learning opportunity where you work together to improve the alignment.
- Find big, engaging challenges for the team to push their skills with.
- Use after action reviews to track and improve on the learning (Chapter Three).

Helping others get plugged in is a spectacular way to continue developing your own expertise. We learn to frame the material in new ways when we teach others. This gives us a richer set of experiences and lenses to use ourselves.

••••••••••••••••••••••••••

We've looked at some ways to help your teammates get on the same page. Now what? I see this as saving the best for last.

"May you live in interesting times." A March 25, 2009, Wikipedia entry noted that a possible origin of this Chinese saying (or curse) is the proverb *shí shì zào yīng xióng,* or "The times produce their heroes."[24] These times are offering us the opportunity to be heroes in our organizations. In Part Two I'll highlight some of what I see as the biggest and best areas to address.

part
TWO

Learning to Plug In

I n Part One I presented the three practices of plugged-in management: Stop-Look-Listen, Mixing, and Sharing. Stop-Look-Listen is a reflective practice that should be engaged throughout all your organizational design work. Stop and see what the needs and opportunities are. Mix together a powerful, appropriately balanced combination of technology, organization, and people. Share plugged-in practices so that they become the model for how the rest of your organization and associations manage—as a result, plugging in will become easier for all.

In Part Two I focus on your personal ability to plug in and offer suggestions and tools for developing your current abilities into something even more powerful. The chapters here model the ideas from Part One. In Chapter Six you stop, look, and listen in the context of your personal practice. In Chapter Seven you get the opportunity to practice mixing by working through some real-world examples. In Chapter Eight I provide an in-depth case from which you can learn the power of plugged-in management when it is applied throughout the organization.

Part Two acknowledges the difficulty of organizational change and the importance of being plugged in in real-world situations with competing ways of looking at things and needs for resources. Wolf Cramer's perspective on finding the right balance for the situation highlights (1) how reality can be an excellent teacher and (2) the value that plugged-in viewpoints can create when driving change in a modern organization.[1]

Finding the Right Balance for the Situation

Wolf Cramer uses plugged-in practices every day as a business transformation consultant within IBM's CIO organization. He serves on the board of IBM's intrapreneur contest program (iFund), and he's been recognized as a "Master Catalyst" for helping innovative ideas get developed into prototypes. He has also supported more traditional customer relationship management (CRM) systems used within IBM. As he describes it, IBM's CIO organization has three towers that support internal adoption of technology tools and work practices: the Innovation tower, the Transformation tower, and the Run tower. Wolf works in the Transformation tower, helping make decisions about which innovations should be passed on to day-to-day operations and how that transformation can best proceed.

Asked how his perspective on plugged-in management has evolved over time, this successful information technology professional immediately began to speak of people:

> I've become more sensitive and aware of the interrelationship of people, process, and technology with respect to achieving goals and deriving value. I've learned that how you adjust one part has implications for the others. Even if there's something that has obvious value, such as technology improvements, there's an element of people and corporate culture that's averse to change. This aversion, if not considered and addressed, can undermine the overall

value of the transformation. Awareness of how significant these impacts can be is something that you come to get greater and greater understanding of over time.

What may be obvious to me is not obvious to others, and the new idea may be disruptive to what other people know and how they react. Fear of change is much more significant than I would have thought. If I've matured, it's in knowing that the people elements of managing change are extremely complex and will make or break your efforts if not addressed.

There is a balance in Wolf's approach. Even while his sound foundations in technology continue to grow, he has balanced these with greater focus on the people portions of organizational work. Many of the plugged-in managers I've met show this progression from one area of strength to many. Wolf also touched on plugged-in shortcomings he's seen:

I often see very sharp focus on process and technology impacts of a change. There's great rigor applied to system inputs and outputs, financial and human resources needed, and even technical models of the changes and project dependencies. Unfortunately, too often the scrutiny is focused on tangible elements of an effort and little sensitivity is shown around the motivations that drive people to make change and adopt new things.

His summary of these issues is vivid:

In order to take advantage of new technology or process improvement, if I had $100 I would spend $30 on technology, $20 on process, and $50 on people. Without the people adopting, you get very limited value or return.

Oftentimes people focus on delivering on time and on budget. IT guys like me come in, and our project's success is typically based on our ability to manage scope, time, and budget. I know what to put inside the box and when I need to deliver the box. But perhaps the business isn't doing a good job at teaching people how to use what's inside the box, explaining why that tool is important to strategy and the company, or providing financial or nonfinancial incentives so people use these great capabilities. So I did everything on time, but it didn't stimulate the adoption. Business value is derived from people using stuff, not stuff being delivered on time.

I won't argue that Wolf's $30-$20-$50 distribution of "attention" is appropriate for everyone. Just as different cuisines have different proportions for their foundational ingredient mix, it is the same for different organizations and contexts. For Wolf's setting, experience shows this is a good foundational balance. As you think about developing your own plugged-in practice, consider the appropriate mix in your own setting. What distribution of attention have you seen in successful versus less successful transformations?

There's also the issue of impediments or barriers to consider. To be able to mix the dimensions of people, technology tools, and organizational processes, you have to first be able to see and, from Wolf's perspective, have room for your options:

As an IT professional, the largest barrier I have to overcome to be more plugged in is understanding the context and goals of the people leveraging the output of my work. Costs and business case justification can be challenging, but developing empathy to understand how something fits into a person's routine is exceedingly difficult but important. How will they use a new tool or practice? What is the trade-off for the users? Is what I am delivering a substitute for something else?

Another element to understanding the context of people is knowing how they will perceive your offering. There are many systems and processes required in a typical modern

organization. Then add in the creativity and innovation of
your staff and even more optional capabilities become
available. In IBM we have so much choice that it becomes
overwhelming. I might just be looking for a hammer, but
when I open up the IBM garage, it's wall-to-wall tools. I can't
find just a hammer. It requires focus and energy to find
what I need, so I just give up. I need some white space so I
can make sense out of what's going on around me, and if
it's too noisy, I return to what I know rather than embrace
something new.

Wolf's comments suggest that even when you do stop, look, and listen, the situation may be too noisy to learn anything about the situation. Less can be more—but how do you steel yourself to keep the simple view, while also not overlooking exceptional opportunities? This is a challenge for all of us as we develop our plugged-in practice. Look for ways of cutting through the noise in the real-world scenarios provided in the examples that follow. This is a way of developing a form of plugged-in practice that will be more powerful in your particular organization.

By providing Wolf's insights, I feel like I'm giving away the answers to the assessment tool in the next chapter. However, we don't all start with Wolf's strength in the technology dimension of plugged-in management's technology, organization, and people mix. In the chapters that follow, think about your own balance of skills and how they can be improved, or at least how you can use an awareness of your biases as you consider options for change.

chapter
SIX

Assess Your Ability to Plug In

W e have all developed some level of savvy about how best to mix together people, technology, and organizational process within particular contexts to thrive in today's environment. For example, you probably take into account an organization's available tools and processes, as well as a group's membership and skills, as you think about how to collaborate. To the extent that you do this effectively, efficiently, and creatively, you have greater expertise in plugging in.

Many of the plugged-in managers I talk to do not see themselves as unique. They seem to simply see a need to manage in a particular way (which just happens to be the plugged-in way), and they do it. These managers mix together the technology, organizational, and people components for better performance— focusing not just on one small change but rather on overall design, often as second nature.

For those of you working on enhancing your skill in plugging in, it is useful to be more conscious about what you are doing and how far you have to go to become a true expert.

How Plugged In Are You?

The interviews and research I have done for this book allow me to see trends across plugged-in managers' backgrounds. Here, I've used those interviews to build a personal audit tool based on scenarios like the one at the beginning of Chapter One. I designed this tool to help executives, managers, and individual contributors, all of us, evaluate our business practice in terms of plugged-in management: working with all three dimensions of technology, organizations, and people—simultaneously. We want to use all three in planning, and we want to implement change with all three.

Consider each of the following scenarios, including the one we first saw in Chapter One.[1] Each scenario was developed from an interview with a plugged-in manager and then refined during my sessions with a broad range of managers. The idea was to develop outcomes for the scenarios that could signal different levels and types of savvy. The scenarios cover topics from social media to teleconferencing and cross-functions from customer service to software design.

As you consider your responses to each scenario, stay in the role. If the scenario says you are an engineer, be the best plugged-in engineer you can imagine. If the scenario says you are an executive in a high-tech start-up, think about what that might be like and answer the questions from that perspective. There are no right or wrong answers—even the people in the interviews saw many different approaches to each problem. What you are trying to do is apply plugged-in management as best you can. In Chapter Seven, I will outline how you can link your results to opportunities to improve your own skill in plugging in.

Customer Service Scenario

Effectiveness Ranking Key

1	2	3	4	5	6	7
Extremely Ineffective	Ineffective	Somewhat Ineffective	Neither Ineffective nor Effective	Somewhat Effective	Effective	Extremely Effective

You are an executive at an online retailing company. A mid-level customer service representative at your company has begun tracking and responding to customer comments on Facebook and Twitter without clearing his actions with management. The response from customers has been great, and you've even gotten some popular press coverage. But this isn't a sanctioned activity. What is your best response? Referring to the effectiveness ranking key, please enter the number for the effectiveness ranking that most closely matches your opinion of each response.

A. _____ Contact the service rep and ask him to stop until you've had a chance to clear this approach with company security and marketing.

B. _____ Contact the service rep and congratulate him on the great idea. Let other executives know about the service representative's success.

C. _____ Add a computer monitoring tool to keep track of the customer service rep activities on this public site. Get involved only if you see a problem building.

D. _____ Write a new company policy about employee actions on social media sites.

E. _____ Organize and train a team of customer service reps to help the first service rep as public interest grows. Have this team suggest guidelines and tools for other areas of the organization to use.

F. _____ Automatically block access to social networking sites from company computers.

China–U.S. Team Scenario

Effectiveness Ranking Key						
1	2	3	4	5	6	7
Extremely Ineffective	Ineffective	Somewhat Ineffective	Neither Ineffective nor Effective	Somewhat Effective	Effective	Extremely Effective

Your group is taking on a complex new innovation project, but you don't have access to enough people locally (Western United States) to succeed. Your best partner location is in China. China has engineers who have the skill set you need, are excited about the technology you are working on, and represent an important new market for your finished product. For this environment, rate each approach to organizing the team and the work.

A. _____ Break the project down into tightly defined pieces for which clear start and finish metrics can be identified. Have small, collocated teams work on the tightly defined pieces and assemble all of them at the end.

B. _____ Have one location do the design and prototyping and the other location do the quality assessment and evaluation.

C. _____ Create subteams with engineers from both the United States and China. Give these subteams tightly defined projects; then put them all together at the end.

D. _____ Create one team consisting of all the engineers at both locations. Give responsibility for the whole project to a single team, but let subgroups emerge. Convene face-to-face, full-team meetings every six months. Use video-conferencing and smaller trips between the full-team meetings.

Bank Scenario						
Effectiveness Ranking Key						
1	2	3	4	5	6	7
Extremely Ineffective	Ineffective	Somewhat Ineffective	Neither Ineffective nor Effective	Somewhat Effective	Effective	Extremely Effective

You are a professional management consultant. A good friend of yours has taken a new management job at a major bank. The 350 employees in her group do back-office processing of loan materials, which is not going well. Mistakes are made, and conversations with salespeople (who originate the paperwork) often result in yelling. They are about to adopt a multimillion-dollar workflow technology, so your friend has called you for advice. Her perception is that there is no creativity or motivation in the bank, and she jokes that she'd like to fire them all, but HR won't let her. Rate the following approaches in terms of how likely they are to improve the loan processing activity.

A. _____   Get HR to agree to fire them all, and start over with new employees.

B. _____   Put the technology adoption on hold. Work with a subset of the employees and salespeople via workshops on workflow and systems thinking.

C. _____   Implement the workflow technology, given your best analysis of how the work should be done, and provide extensive training on how to use it accurately.

D. _____   Add five loan processing employees to the workflow technology implementation team.

E. _____   Hire five loan processing employees from your competitor, where a similar implementation has already been successful.

Facilitation Scenario

Effectiveness Ranking Key

1	2	3	4	5	6	7
Extremely Ineffective	Ineffective	Somewhat Ineffective	Neither Ineffective nor Effective	Somewhat Effective	Effective	Extremely Effective

Your organization makes its living by facilitating agreement across diverse stakeholder groups. The organization spends between three and five million dollars a year in technology infrastructure: online meeting tools, voting tools, and automated dissemination of documents. It takes an average of fifteen months for stakeholder groups to come to agreement (prior to the implementation of all this technology, it took an average of sixty months). Your next project will include twenty different organizations across five countries. Rate each collaboration approach based on how effectively it supports speed and solidarity.

A. _____   Face-to-face meetings only.

B. _____   Face-to-face meetings at critical points: Use online collaboration tools before and after the face-to-face meetings.

C. _____   All votes done face-to-face; all other work completed online.

D. _____   Face-to-face for everyone who can physically get to the meeting; all others can use the teleconferencing tools.

E. _____   Face-to-face if 100 percent of the stakeholders can physically get to the meeting; if even one person can't attend face-to-face, then the whole meeting will be held electronically.

F. _____   Majority rules: face-to-face or teleconferencing for each meeting—whichever the majority prefers.

How You Compare

Compare your answers to those of expert plugged-in managers and other people in general. The plugged-in managers are noted as PIM in the graphs. The answers from the general population are noted as GP. I've left spots for you to plot your own responses too, above the Y marks. The dotted lines between the GP answers and the PIM answers show how the responses between the two populations compare. The plugged-in and general population ratings are averages. There are no "right" or "wrong" answers; rather, the idea is to see whether you can determine why plugged-in managers might rate the particular choice the same as or differently than you did.

For each scenario, rather than discussing each individually, after briefly describing the overall results I will focus on the responses that seem to show the most difference between those identified as experts in plugged-in management and the general population. These "separating" responses are the ones noted with asterisks on the results charts. Generally the difference is in the formality of the mix—the plugged-in managers seem to be more comfortable with letting the final mix develop from the situation rather than specifying a specific recipe. Plugged-in managers seem to score more emergent responses higher and more control-focused responses lower than do people who have not been identified as plugged-in managers. Plugged-in managers also seem to select answers that draw on more complex solutions rather than choosing solutions focused on just people, or technology tools, or organizational processes.

Customer Service Scenario

I'll start with the example from the very beginning of the book: the customer service scenario in which the customer service representative is responding to customers via social media tools like Facebook and Twitter. As Figure 6.1 illustrates, people in general

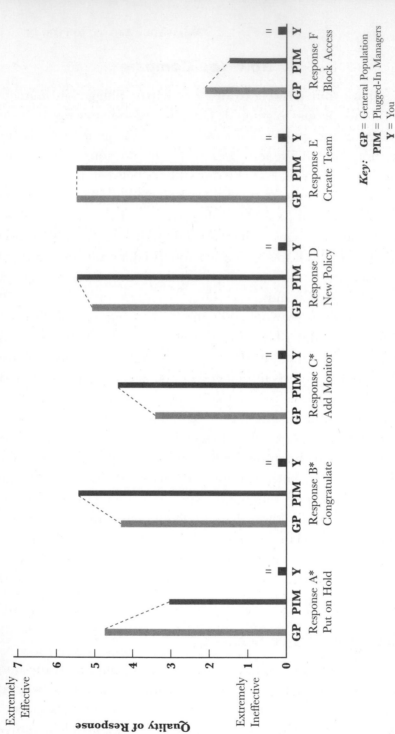

Figure 6.1 Responses to Customer Service Scenario

Quality of Response

Extremely Effective 7

Extremely Ineffective 1

Response A*
Put on Hold

Response B*
Congratulate

Response C*
Add Monitor

Response D
New Policy

Response E
Create Team

Response F
Block Access

GP PIM Y

Key: **GP** = General Population
PIM = Plugged-In Managers
Y = You

* Responses showing the greatest difference between plugged-in managers and the general population.

126

think that Response D, having a new social media policy, is a good idea, as is Response E, setting up collaborative training to support the activity. Response F, automatically blocking social media websites, is seen by everyone as the worst response. Plugged-in managers differ from the general population in giving higher marks to Response B, congratulating and publicizing the representative's success, and Response C, using a technology monitoring tool but not getting involved unless there is a problem; and in giving lower marks to Response A, stopping the customer service rep from using social media until security and marketing have said it is all right.

How do your answers compare? If your image of the best approach is one in which you celebrate the representative's success while balancing the risk with a solid policy and training program—and perhaps an automatic monitoring system, lightly deployed—you match closely with the plugged-in managers I have met. Most plugged-in managers are intrigued by the representative's ingenuity and motivation to help the customers wherever the customers can be found. They also understand that a solid social media policy and training system will help all employees understand the boundaries of these new technologies in organizational practice. Electronic monitoring support may be necessary to protect the organization and maintain awareness of how things are going, and this support doesn't have to be implemented as Big Brother.

If you were more inclined to put the brakes on the use of social media in this case, ask yourself why you would do so. Again, there are no right or wrong answers; these scenarios can't describe the full situation and context, and they may not match your industry's required practice.[2] If you felt that stopping the practice until you had more information was the best approach, be sure you had reasons that would outweigh the downside of stopping an innovative approach that seemed to be working at least in the areas of customer satisfaction and public relations. Might there be ways to hold on to the positives while avoiding the risks you see if you leveraged all of your technology tools, organizational processes, and people?

China–U.S. Team Scenario

The plugged-in responses in the China–U.S. team scenario follow a similar "emergence is good" pattern. In this scenario there is a complex innovation project that requires an international team to staff it. As shown in Figure 6.2, both plugged-in managers and the general population think that Response D, establishing one team and allowing subgroups to emerge, is the best, although the plugged-in managers rate its effectiveness over a full point higher than do members of the general population. The Response A rankings are interesting: The general population rates this control-focused choice, breaking the project into tightly defined pieces, as the second best option; the plugged-in managers rate it as the worst. In a similar contrast, the plugged-in managers give their second-best rating to Response C, giving full responsibility to one team for design and prototyping, and full authority for quality to the other team; the general population rates this as the least effective option.

Why would expert plugged-in managers be more comfortable with this freedom in the organization, while those who are less plugged in are not? In general, experts collect more cues when they make judgments of situations—they have a more detailed perspective and perhaps then have more confidence that they'll notice if something starts to go wrong.[3] Think about novice cooks and expert cooks. The novice is likely to follow the recipe word for word; the expert may use the recipe only as inspiration.

Compare your responses with those of the plugged-in managers. Did you feel pressure to build a single team rather than multiple teams? Multiple teams would require greater control so that their finished products could effectively be combined, but would such teams perform at the same level as a single team, given

Figure 6.2 Responses to China–U.S. Team Scenario

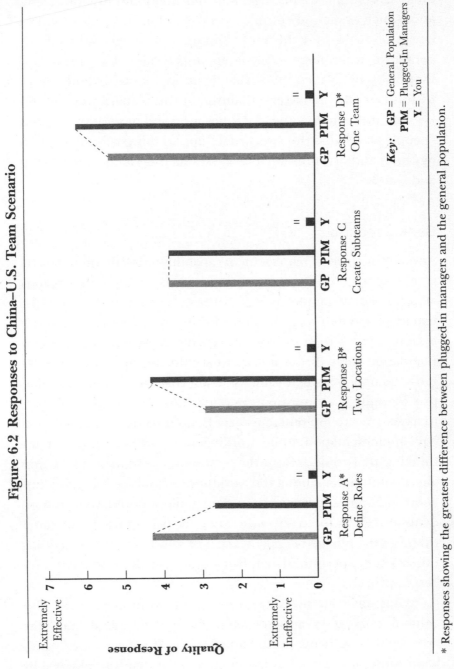

Key: **GP** = General Population
      PIM = Plugged-In Managers
      Y = You

* Responses showing the greatest difference between plugged-in managers and the general population.

greater room for self-management? It's important to look at situations such as these as complex settings with many trade-offs. The key is often to find the most important leverage point—be it people, a technology tool, or an organizational process—and then work to balance the trade-offs using the other dimensions. In this case, the manager who inspired this scenario focused on keeping the team together for innovation and motivation reasons (people issues) and then worked to support this goal with technology tools and organizational processes such as videoconferencing and travel.

Bank Scenario

Another plugged-in management capability visible in these results is the experts' willingness to manage or mix multiple dimensions at once. For example, in the bank scenario (see Figure 6.3), expert plugged-in managers give low marks to Response D, the option to just hire more loan processing employees. The general population rates this as a somewhat effective approach. Simply hiring people is a single-dimension approach—an organizational process only. The two responses rated "Effective" by the plugged-in managers are multidimensional: B, holding off on the technology implementation while working on workflow and systems thinking that could inform the technology design; and C, going ahead and implementing the workflow technology but providing good training at the same time. The general population respondents also think these responses are effective but not to the same extent as the plugged-in managers. The good news is that neither novices nor experts think that firing everyone (Response A) is the best approach.

What was your thinking as you made your selections? The general population answers make good basic sense and may even be seen as being more cost-effective. If your answers paralleled those of the general population more than the plugged-in

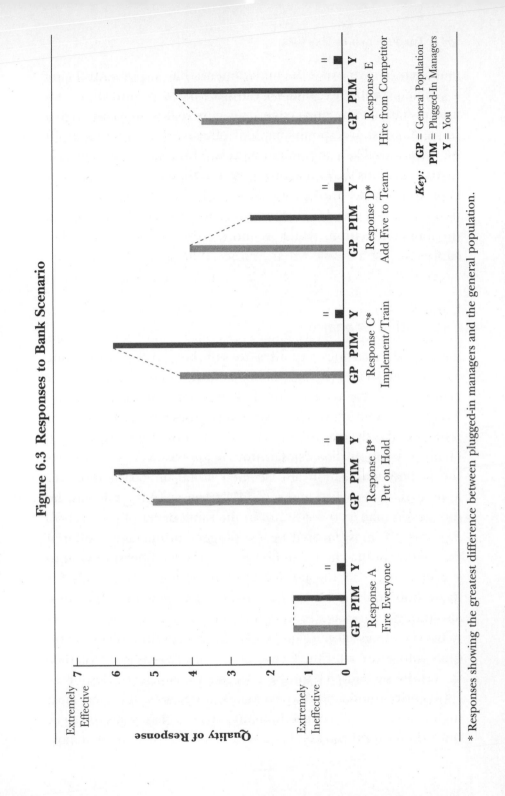

Figure 6.3 Responses to Bank Scenario

Key: **GP** = General Population
PIM = Plugged-In Managers
Y = You

* Responses showing the greatest difference between plugged-in managers and the general population.

managers, did you view the multidimensional responses as being too much trouble to go to for the anticipated result? Here's my interpretation: The plugged-in managers realize that although a single-dimension response may look effective and easier to implement, it is less likely to result in success. This is key. Many changes in organizations look great on paper, and their outcomes, like this new workflow technology, make logical sense for the organization's goals—*if* they are successfully implemented. The trick is in the implementation, which is more likely to be successful if supported by a whole-system, rather than a single-dimension, approach.

Facilitation Scenario

Figure 6.4, charting responses to our last scenario—the one focused on facilitating agreement among different stakeholder groups—gives you a picture of (1) how plugged-in managers gain a degree of comfort with letting the outcomes emerge rather than trying to tightly control them, and (2) how they are able to combine multiple dimensions into one approach. To their credit, the general population also seemed to be on board with this approach, as their first and second choices were the same as the plugged-in managers'—just not in the same order of preference. Response D, most favored by the plugged-in managers, offered face-to-face as the choice for everyone who could physically get to the meeting, with the possibility of teleconferencing tools for those who could not meet face-to-face. The general population also thought this was a solid option but chose Response B—face-to-face meetings at critical points, with use of online collaboration tools before and after the face-to-face meetings—as their top pick (it was the second pick for the plugged-in managers). Responses F (majority rules) and A (face-to-face only) were the next most highly rated by the plugged-in managers, whereas C was the clear third choice for the general population. I can assure you that most

Figure 6.4 Responses to Facilitation Scenario

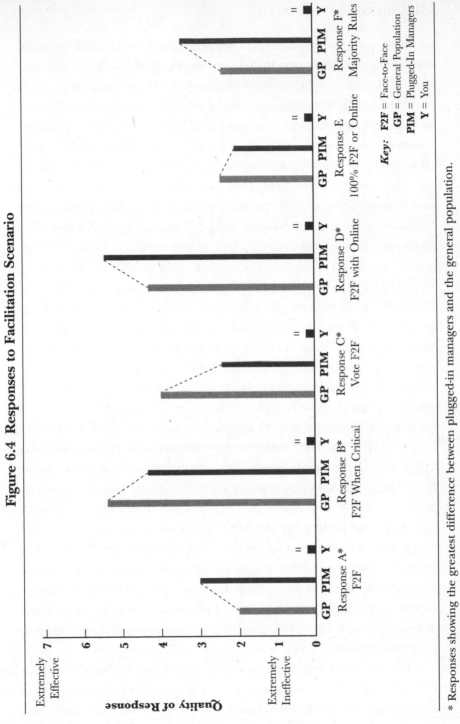

Quality of Response

Extremely Effective 7

6

5

4

3

2

1 Extremely Ineffective

0

GP PIM Y
Response A*
F2F

GP PIM Y
Response B*
F2F When Critical

GP PIM Y
Response C*
Vote F2F

GP PIM Y
Response D*
F2F with Online

GP PIM Y
Response E
100% F2F or Online

GP PIM Y
Response F*
Majority Rules

Key: **F2F** = Face-to-Face
GP = General Population
PIM = Plugged-In Managers
Y = You

* Responses showing the greatest difference between plugged-in managers and the general population.

133

of these plugged-in managers are also experts in collaboration technology, but because of their broad plugging-in expertise, they have a bias toward face-to-face work when it is possible and when it fits the needs of the group. The key to their plugged-in practices is that they understand the costs and benefits of their different options; their decisions are then based on providing the best possible mix of options, including decisions being made by the group.

The options for how best to hold a complex meeting are themselves complex. In this instance, consider putting less focus on how your choices matched; instead, consider how the decision was made. In this scenario, travel costs can be significant. So too are the outcomes of the meeting. Face-to-face communication will likely allow for better transfer of information,[4] but is it worth the cost of perhaps limiting the number or diversity of the people who could attend? In this particular example, the facilitation leader wanted an international perspective in the discussions and speed and solidarity around the results. Some form of electronic communication was required to meet these goals, given travel costs and individual participants' availability. Did you weigh formal costs (such as travel) against time, and the ability to reach agreement over electronic versus face-to-face communication channels? If you made your decisions based on a starting point like "electronic communication (that is, online collaboration or teleconferencing) could work *if* . . ." and then came up with strategies for increasing the facilitation effort or increasing the engagement of the group members, you were showing plugged-in expertise like that of our respondents. Their plugged-in practice came in the form of balancing the costs and benefits of the different communication modes with an understanding of the participants and different organizational processes for supporting communication.

The scenario approach is a rich way to think about the practice of plugged-in management. In Chapter Seven I will use the responses here to help you focus on strategies that may help you improve. Also, www.ThePluggedInManager.com will update available scenarios over time and keep track of how experts and a more general population respond. Feel free to contribute new scenarios on the site. You may have noticed clear differences between how plugged-in managers and non-plugged-in managers act in your own setting; share your experiences, and we can start collecting comparison data in other organizations.

Quick and Dirty

Before we go on, I want to offer a simpler and faster approach to assessing how plugged in you are. When I have a group that doesn't have the time to consider all the scenarios, or I don't have the luxury of being able to interpret the scenario responses, I offer people a self-assessment form (see Worksheet 6.5 on page 136). The introduction is like the one for the scenarios in that there are no right or wrong answers and honesty is the best policy.

It turns out that this simpler approach is a rough predictor of how people answer on the scenarios. Self-assessments of six and seven are common for people who tend to answer like our identified expert plugged-in managers.

You can also think of the nine short survey items as goals. If you aren't answering with sixes and sevens, this is something you can strive for—and as you do, you can look forward to seeing great outcomes in your organization as a result.

• •

The next step is to use the information from these assessments to guide your continued development of your personal ability to plug in. Even if you have mastered the ability to mix technology, organization, and people, every situation is unique and requires a thoughtful strategy. In the next chapter I will show how some expert and not-so-expert managers have addressed complicated situations.

Short-Form Plugged-In Self-Assessment

1	2	3	4	5	6	7
Totally False	Largely False	Somewhat False	As Likely to Be True as False	Somewhat True	Largely True	Absolutely True

There are no right or wrong answers to these questions. Please respond with your best judgment. Try to think of specific examples from your own experience that match the situation and answer related to what actually happened.

Statements	Rating
When I adopt a new technology, I always consider other changes in my work flow that might help.	
Other people come to me for advice on how to implement organizational changes that include a technology tool.	
I always consider the technology changes we will have to make if we adopt a particular organizational change.	
I always look for changes to organizational processes that could be improved with a technology tool.	
I always consider what organizational changes are necessary to get the benefits of a proposed technology tool.	
I always look for adjustments to technology implementations that may not fit our organization.	
When I adopt a change in my work flow, I always consider technology changes that might help in combination.	
Other people come to me for advice on how to integrate technology tools into our organizational setting.	

chapter
SEVEN

Plugging In Through Practice

Each of the scenarios in Chapter Six is the result of an interview in which I asked a plugged-in manager (so described by their peers) to tell me about a time when the manager had to mix together people, technology tools, and organizational process—in a way that the manager couldn't have learned from a book, given that this book didn't exist! Their situations covered completely new technologies (social media), traditional organizational change (adjustments to work flow), modern global organizational design, and other common management concerns.

Broadly speaking, those scenarios and the answers of a variety of plugged-in managers suggest that the ability to plug in emerges over time and eventually results in a thoughtful mix of a deep understanding of human capabilities and needs, technology tool use, and organizational process development. The plugged-in practices I presented in Part One—Stop-Look-Listen, Mixing, and Sharing—are a way of thinking about how new designs and strategies emerge and how they can be supported throughout their development.

You had the chance in Chapter Six to compare your responses to those of plugged-in managers. In this chapter you'll have a chance to think about some additional scenarios, but this time not with multiple-choice answers. The idea is to consider a situation, take a moment or two to consider a plugged-in response, and then read on to see what happened in the real setting.

Use the feedback from your responses in Chapter Six to make adjustments in this section. Reflect on the three practices of a plugged-in manager:

○ *Stop-Look-Listen* (the ability to assess your environment and available options). *Stop* to reflect on the situation. *Look* at available data (or collect some via simple experiments) to narrow down the possibilities. *Listen* to feedback from others involved at the core and in connecting roles.

If your highest-rated scenario responses were decisive, but perhaps therefore limited in their scope, you may want to put additional attention into your practice of Stop-Look-Listen. Taking time to let the situation develop and be understood is a practice that supports emergence.

○ *Mix* solutions that balance the people involved with the technology tools and organizational practice. Think about negotiation—how can you negotiate a solution built of people, technology tools, and organizational process? Multiple solutions are possible, but each must appropriately balance across the three dimensions for the situation you found in the assessment.

If your highest-rated scenario responses focused on a single lever, rather than a full system of solutions, you may find value in returning to the practice of mixing. It is rare that a complex problem has a simple solution. There may be a strong focus on one of the technology, organization, or people dimensions, but there should be supporting moves or consideration of the other two dimensions as well.[1]

○   *Share* this approach with the people you live and work with, largely through publicly modeling how you plug in through your own actions and giving others the chance to gain experience in plugging in. The more you share, the more the mixing process will become commonplace in your teams and organizations.

The short self-report assessment in Chapter Six provides a subtle look into the practice of sharing. Consider your response to the two items that ask about whether others come to you for advice on organizational and technology changes. If people are already coming to you for advice, you are engaged in the sharing practice. Consider whether or not your sharing includes outreach as well as being responsive to requests for help. If you aren't being approached, consider how you could make yourself more visible and proactive as a resource.

Amazon's Kindle eBook Reader

Amazon, the online retailer, provides us with an example of the flexibility of modern technologies—for better or for worse—and how being plugged in can help. Amazon has had great success with offering their Kindle, a physical eBook reader that can download electronic versions of books. They also offer applications to read these electronic versions on your computer, smart-phone, or tablet computer. You buy (technically, you license) an electronic book from Amazon, just like you'd buy a hard copy book but without the shipping. You surf to the Amazon website, choose the Kindle edition as the form of the book you'd like to buy, and it automatically appears in your Kindle or Kindle application.[2]

Amazon also allows others to sell copies of books using the Amazon website. This is like eBay allowing you to sell your merchandise using eBay's website. You own the merchandise, but they facilitate the transaction.

In July of 2009, Amazon became aware that a version of George Orwell's book *1984* had been posted to the Amazon website by a third-party publisher that did not own the rights to the book. Many people had bought this particular version and had downloaded it to their Kindle eBook reader and applications. Amazon was in a tough position. They had facilitated a fraudulent purchase and had to decide what to do.

• •
WHAT WOULD YOU DO?

Amazon runs the website that facilitates finding books to buy, the payment process (for both buyers and sellers), the download process, communication with the customers, and automatic updates to the Kindle. This gives them a variety of options.

Thinking as a plugged-in manager, apply the three practices of plugged-in management and decide what to do.

• •

What Happened?

Without warning, Amazon remotely deleted copies of George Orwell's novel *1984* from nearly two thousand customers' Kindle eBooks.[3]

This incident illustrates how technologies, especially tightly intertwined ones, are complex and often in flux. After the book's true rights holder notified Amazon, Amazon took the book down from the Amazon website and proceeded to remotely delete the copies from customers' Kindles. Both actions are examples of a purely technical response.

The result was a huge backlash from the Kindle community. How truly ironic that the book in question was *1984*! The press had a field day comparing this action with the book's authoritarian themes.

Like many modern organizational business models, the Amazon strategy for the Kindle eBook engages multiple organizations using sophisticated technology to create the Kindle ecosystem. This ecosystem is interwoven of enthusiastic users, technology, and organizational process. Given this complexity, plugged-in managers need all of their abilities to see and work with technical and organizational options in a human context. In this instance, Amazon seemed initially to have dealt with the problem only via technology, with little regard for organizational or people issues.

The Kindle owners had not realized that the technology that gave them automatic access to their purchased electronic books also allowed for remote deletion. According to *The New York Times*, Amazon's own Terms of Service agreement for the Kindle grants customers the permanent right to the material purchased; this Terms of Service agreement underscores that although Amazon has the technical ability to delete books (using the same technology that synchronizes customers' purchases across their Kindles and PCs), they did not create an expectation that it could happen.[4]

As a result, Amazon has revised its approach. The *New York Times* report quotes an Amazon spokesman: "We are changing our systems so that in the future we will not remove books from customers' devices in these circumstances."

It's a constant dance. Amazon surprised its users with a technology feature the users didn't like. The response was dramatic because people don't like things they've paid for to disappear. Amazon was able to move quickly to respond to user feedback by changing the system so it would not happen again. I don't believe Amazon has specified whether this is a technology fix, an organizational policy change, or both. From a plugged-in management perspective, it doesn't matter. What is important for plugged-in managers is to understand their options, to pick a strategy that makes the best use of all the dimensions, and to make sure that they haven't created unanticipated tensions.

In this case, Amazon is surely making an organizational change of some sort: They are changing their organizational policy about what to do in this setting, they are likely tying the policy into the technology infrastructure to support the policy, and they are advertising the policy shift so that the people involved, customers and Amazon employees and vendors, are aware of the policy change. Their initial response may not have been plugged in, but it seems their recovery process has been. If they learned from the experience, then I expect their managers are more plugged in and in tune with their people, technology, and organizations than they were before the event. The flexibility of their technology was both the cause and part of the solution to their error. It was easy to delete the books, but it was harder to manage organizational policy and user expectations.

Plugged-in management speaks to all the functions of the organization. In Amazon's case, you can see the impact on product design (the entire Amazon/Kindle ecosystem) and public relations.

Nucor: Extreme Plugged-In Management at All Levels

To my eyes, two of the most fascinating sights to behold are hot metal in motion and a group of people in headlong pursuit of a shared purpose. Those images are the essence of Nucor.

—Ken Iverson, legendary past president and CEO of Nucor[5]

Nucor is both the largest producer of steel in the United States and North America's largest recycler. They've never had a layoff at any of their steel mills, and since their inception in 1966 they have had only three unprofitable quarters (the first three quarters of 2009). Nucor is known for the innovative capabilities of its teammates (employees), the quality and value of its steel, and the safety of its facilities. A main section of the Nucor website is devoted to telling their story, including describing Nucor's unique culture:

- Safety First
- Eliminating Hierarchy
- Granting Trust and Freedom
- Giving All Workers a Stake in the Company
- Turning Everyone into a Decision Maker
- Inspiring a Work Ethic
- Employee Relations Principles

These culture components intertwine to form the strength of their approach. For example, their famous "pay for team performance" model couldn't work if the teams didn't have the power to make decisions related to the performance of their team. Decision making couldn't work as well as it does if there were numerous layers of management; at Nucor, there are only four. This is plugged-in management, built steadily from the 1960s to today. Innovative steel production is what they do, but they manage the technology in a way that is tightly bound to their organizational processes. They mix together the technology tools and organizational process, and are very focused on the people in their organization.

From their website:

> Push decision-making down to the lowest
> level . . . 'empowerment' has gone beyond a corporate
> buzzword, and become a way of life at Nucor: From
> employees who are unafraid to stop production whenever
> they see a potential problem; to front-line workers who
> regularly spend time at their customer's facility to get a
> better idea of how to improve quality; to employees who
> take it upon themselves to create new and better ways to
> produce steel.[6]

There are multiple books describing Nucor's approach to business. One of the most famous is *Plain Talk: Lessons from a*

Business Maverick, by the founding CEO, Ken Iverson.[7] Written in 1997, it is full of three decades of examples of plugged-in management. Nucor's strong ability to mix together people, technology tools, and organizational practice is alive and well. Three Nucor executives—Dan Krug, director of human resources and organizational development at Nucor headquarters; Doyle Hopper, general manager of Nucor's Vulcraft Group and Nucor Cold Finish in Nebraska; and Dirk Petersen, Nucor Steel, Nebraska—took the time to tell me about recent vivid examples.[8]

A Plugged-In Response to Adversity: Nucor and the Vulcraft Flood

In June of 2010 the Norfolk, Nebraska area, home to four Nucor divisions, was struck by horrible flooding. A tragic outcome of this flood was a railroad bridge collapse, killing one of the three Nebraska Central Railroad employees involved in an inspection. The bridge outage diverted the river water, increasing the flooding at Nucor's Vulcraft site and cutting part of the transportation link for raw materials and finished goods at another.

I'll first ask you to consider how you might have dealt with the Vulcraft flooding; later, you'll have a chance to consider your options for overcoming the critical transportation issue caused by the bridge outage.

• •
WHAT WOULD YOU DO?

By 3 P.M. Nucor's Vulcraft site was underwater: two inches deep in the offices, two feet deep inside the plant. The majority of the plant's equipment runs underground, and the electrical network is substantial.

Thinking as a plugged-in manager with Nucor values and experience, what do you do?

• •

What Happened?

In true Nucor style, the plant never stopped moving product, and their customers had no delays. While other local firms sent their employees home and hired contractors to deal with the mess, the Nucor plant stayed open, continued to provide for customers, and the teammates put themselves back online. Here's the Nucor approach, from Doyle Hopper: "Limit damage. Save the plant." He observed: "Who better to do the job than the people who own it? They're in this together. I don't want somebody else [e.g., contractors] in there fighting the battle. We know the result we're looking for, and we're prepared."

The initial activities were sandbagging and turning off power. The sandbagging involved people from all parts of the facility. From production to office staff in dress clothes, they were out in the rain getting the job done. Doyle said, "Nobody told them to do it. True Nucor people—culture just reacted to situation. I was blown away, but I shouldn't have been. People who weren't sandbagging were moving computers and files on top of desks."

Nobody told them to do it. To me this is decades of plugged-in management giving the Nucor people the ability to assess the situation and realize that a very simple technology could help (sandbags) and that they needed to break away from ordinary work roles and get the job done—safely. They knew the boundaries and quickly worked to mix together a response.

The flood happened on a Tuesday. Over the next few days, the Vulcraft teammates worked on longer-term approaches, Doyle said.

> Folks sprang into action. Sales, engineering, finance, moved their computers into the detailing center that wasn't impacted by flood. One hundred twenty people were relocated to the other building and back online with customers—didn't miss a beat. By Friday the water was

pumped out, new electrical lines and other electric put in place.

Monday morning business was back to normal. Didn't miss a single customer delivery. People took it upon themselves to arrange for material to make it out on trucks for customers who had to have their material immediately. They found a truck and used a forklift with chains [given the mud] to safely load the shipment.

I asked Doyle how these activities were coordinated. The answer was about the design and practice, not about a single leader or even a senior team.

The Cold Finish and Vulcraft sites have over four hundred people. All are broken into teams: production, shipping, receiving, . . . supervisors report to their manager, [managers report to Doyle] . . . it's streamlined, lean, with clear goals. . . . Great thing about Nucor, you don't have to go through a chain of command to make a decision. Really shows when there is adversity/tragedy. People have been taking initiative all along. It's just part of their nature.

The ability to plug in is often developed by experience. Nucor is known for retention of its teammates and for promoting from within. Both are great ways to build plugged-in managers throughout the organization.

The story at the Norfolk Nucor Steel site is exactly the same—long-standing plugged-in management across all the teammates.

Nucor Steel: Transportation Recovery Through Plugged-In Management

Dirk Petersen, general manager of the Nucor Steel plant in Norfolk, Nebraska, and Troy Brooks, sales/shipping manager, were returning from a business trip on June 15. As they transferred at Chicago's Midway airport, Troy got a call from Mark Eichberger, the rail and scrap supervisor, telling him the railroad bridge had gone out. Normally, approximately 20 percent of the scrap they use to make their steel comes in by rail, as well other materials like coal and lime. Fifty percent of their finished product goes out by rail. The rail link would be down for two months.

●●●●●●●●●●●●●●●●●●●●●●●●●●●

WHAT WOULD YOU DO?

Once again, you're a plugged-in manager with Nucor. A can-do attitude can be a lot of help, but it can't rebuild a railroad bridge. What are your options, and how will you implement your plan?

●●●●●●●●●●●●●●●●●●●●●●●●●●●

What Happened?

Says Dirk: "The goal from day one: take care of customers safely."

When they got back to the site, they joined in the ongoing mixing together of technology and organizational process. Transloading, the movement of truck to rail and vice versa, was the key technology at play. Everyone knew they had to find ways to shift the rail transportation to trucking, quickly, and without letting shipping costs go higher than necessary. While Nucor Steel's computer inventory systems could handle the shift from rail to truck, the physical movement of the materials required quick, safe, but large-scale engineering and construction. Transloading sites were established on the other side of the river. This entailed bringing in a sixty-foot-wide gantry crane from Arizona and the creation of new roads to support the transloading (and help with the bridge repair).

According to Dirk, the process was all about relationships. The daily meetings with local officials and stakeholders were about "making sure everybody knew what everybody else was doing and how they were accountable." Basically, sharing in a way that brought all the actors into the Nucor approach.

Long-standing relationships and the ability to reach quick agreements were key to their success. Sister companies, customers, vendors, and local and federal government all came together to push forward the massive construction process and shift in operational strategy. Many were proactive in their offers to help.

- Permits were granted—collaboration with local and federal government
- Shipping hours were increased—collaboration with vendors and customers
- The local road was closed to all but company business—collaboration with local government
- A second gate was added—collaboration with vendors

Those most knowledgeable in the particular areas stepped up and managed the mixing. Because these companies had tight relationships before the flood, they had good understandings of each other's needs and abilities. Dirk summarized the can-do attitude that supported the work: "We just knew we had to do it. We knew we could do it. We didn't hesitate to do it. Focus on taking care of the customer—safely . . . [especially given this was an] out-of-the-ordinary activity."

The deep relationships meant things could happen when they needed to happen. I believe trust also played a role: Given the relationships and knowledge of the Nucor approach, the customers and vendors knew good decisions would be made. Continuing to support these deep relationships, neither Nucor Steel nor Vulcraft passed along the increased transportation costs to their customers.

The result: "We never missed one beat due to lack of scrap [their main raw material] and our scrap inventory actually grew in the last two months."[9]

Both of these Nucor examples highlight an interesting feature of exceptional plugged-in managers and employees: Deep expertise, whether in technology or organizational process, can make the dimensions almost invisible. Some experts have difficulty describing their work; they just do the work naturally, so they may have a hard time describing the separate steps. These experts make the work look easy when it's not. The work flows so smoothly due to years of experience.

Microsoft's Excel for the Mac Project

Talent, especially software talent, is spread worldwide. The virtual work form required to harness this global talent is different from face-to-face work—even with all our fancy technologies and increased experience at working "together apart." Successful virtual work requires explicit mixing of the people, the technology tools, and the organizational processes—in short, plugged-in management.

Stuart DeSpain is the principal program manager lead in the Excel for the Mac group at Microsoft. Stuart, like most plugged-in managers I talk to, is able to see all three categories of his options—people, technology, and organizational process—and then envision how these options could be mixed together for a strong result.

He gave me an example of how they expanded the Excel for the Mac group to meet the needs of the new major product launch. I could see both explicitness and intentionality in how he thought about the group's overall design and practice:

> Virtual work is part of our DNA: For fifteen years the Mac business unit has spanned two locations: Redmond [Microsoft HQ in Washington State] and Silicon Valley [California]. This was not so much a plan, it's just how it happened. So we've built up a lot of comfort with the phone and videoconferencing. That [background] helped us think about building additional capacity abroad. . . .

> We decided that one of the big centers of talent was
> Beijing. Great graduates, eager people. . . . our challenge
> was to set it up right.

• •
WHAT WOULD YOU DO?

There are a variety of ways to organize the actions of a two-site
software development team. As a plugged-in manager, what do
you do to make sure you hit the challenging goals of timeliness
and quality in this situation?

• •

What Happened?

For Stuart, the mixing practice of plugged-in management is
explicit in the group's catch phrase: One Team, Many Places.

> I've observed that when engineering campuses aren't
> located across the street from each other . . . there's a
> desire to treat the [away] campuses as vendors: give them
> specific tasks, throw them over the wall . . . "Call us if there
> is an emergency, otherwise, call us when it's done."
>
> I didn't think that a "vendor" approach would work well for
> us. We really couldn't just box up Excel, as it's an integral
> part of a system; it's part of Office. We wanted to do it
> right. Initially leaders sat down as a group and set out a
> clear vision statement as a collective: One Team, Many
> Places. We use this phrase all the time: presentations,
> meetings . . . hammering that this is what we are. Not Excel
> in Redmond and Excel in Beijing. An Excel team across
> many campuses.

"One Team, Many Places." Catchy phrase—and the key to
effective distributed development success. The phrase acknowledges the role of people in plugged-in management. As humans,

we tend to focus on people who are physically close to us.[10] You have to work at it, be intentional, to focus on people who are afar.

But Stuart and the Excel team didn't only think about the social psychology of the situation. They also carefully considered the role of technology tools and organizational practice.

> We worked hard on how to translate that high-level goal into very specific unifying actions. At every stage—One Team, Many Places. How are we going to deliver that no matter the situation? Travel, teleconferences, other tools . . . We settled on the idea of summits. The idea is to treat it like a trade show. Every six months one side or other would fly—spend a week, like a family reunion, catching up. If there were presentations that one side or other didn't get to see, we'd show them. We're walking into our fourth summit next week.

> Even more impactful are the one-on-one or small group interactions. These lead me to see a lot of benefit to sharing a meal or drink or social experience. Summits included a lot of activity around tech problems, but evening social experiences bond the team so they think of themselves as a single tribe. Our pulse for summits is about every six months. But in a team located in the same hallway you'd see people once a week or daily. . . .

To manage the time between the summits, they focus on individual travel from both locations and high-interaction tele-conferencing. Even the teleconferencing is intentional, not just casual. The team is well aware of how one side could dominate the conversation and that there may be compromises due to bandwidth issues, configuration, the need to use the screen to show software features rather than faces, and so on. There can be a heavy premium for using video, but they think it's worth it; they design practices to manage the complexity. Stuart says, "We made it clear that it's worth fifteen minutes of setup if that's what

it takes. We have a note taker who scribes the meeting and projects the notes as subtitling. In addition, we have an instant messaging conduit—if someone can't interrupt another way, they can
use that."

The note taking and additional instant messaging conduit are
their fallbacks. The team is well aware of the limitations of video-
conferencing and actively manages the process to get keep the
best "pulse" for the team no matter what the communication
mode. They actively mix together the technology, organizational,
and people dimensions of their work and interaction.

I asked Stuart how he knew that they needed to focus on One
Team, Many Places. I could see that he had stopped, looked, and
listened as he considered how to build one team out of two locations; I was interested in what had triggered this plugged-in
practice.

He described how ten years earlier he'd worked on a team
where his group had the role of the smaller, afar portion of a
virtual project—a position similar to that of the China portion of
his current team. The difference was that the "center of decision"
was not at his site. Objectives would be set, then change, then
change again. "We were miserable. We were disconnected from
our own fate."

This negative virtual team experience has been valuable to
Stuart and his current team.

On reflection, Stuart says he came to understand that the
partner company was great in that situation ten years ago, but
the partner company did not yet understand how to work—to
"mix," in our plugged-in terms—with remote campuses. What his
local group thought was an issue of lack of communication given
their remote location really had more to do with the youth of the
partner firm. They were still in a growth mode, which meant
objectives would change. Stuart says, "It had nothing to do with
geography, just their being a new company. If we'd just talked
about it, if we'd gone out for drinks during a visit and just

talked about the mission, if we'd had the single conversation, it would have changed the dynamic."

So, Stuart says, he is always aware of that experience and is sensitive to the fact that the larger portion of the team will always be perceived as "where the good stuff happens" unless there is an intentional effort to be One Team, Many Places.

This example is valuable for the way it shows the development and execution across all three practices. There was an initial phase of Stop-Look-Listen. Stuart then worked to create an effective mix of people, technology, and organization, which was then shared and continues to guide their approach.

eContact at Cisco

Brett Colbert, now vice president of IT strategy and enterprise architecture at NetApp, gave me a great example from his early management career at Cisco. A mentor suggested that Brett take on a new assignment: eContact. The project would give him a bigger role and broad visibility, given the diversity of subteams involved. Brett said yes, but here's what he found as he stopped, looked, and listened: "I started doing some analysis and saw that pretty much every category related to general project management was broken or in the red: quality component that's being managed—No; code being saved with source control—No; right level of exec buy-in or change management—No. After about two months I went back to Andy [the mentor and overall manager] and said, 'Each individual problem is solvable, but all together it's not. It's a death march, and we're way off course.'"

● ●
WHAT WOULD YOU DO?
They were US$20 million into this project at the time. What does a plugged-in manager do?

● ●

What Happened?

"I was afraid you were going to say that," Andy told Brett. "I agree with you. A rare occurrence, but we have to stop."

Brett continues:

> If you were talk to each person individually they'd say yes, kill it. But when you brought people together there was this strong desire to meet the culture of stretch goals that's embedded at Cisco. People could not resist but to say, "We can fix anything! We can do anything!"
>
> Even the most rational people, when you tried to put the brakes on things, pushed back—even though deep down they knew it wasn't fixable. It was a big epiphany for me in terms of the desire for people to be able to prove or stay on course with these incredible stretch goals. They lose the ability to judge what's reasonable, what's impossible, what's stretch [doable, but challenging].

Brett thought hard about ways to mix things differently for a different result. To everyone's credit, they did not throw good money after bad and escalate their investment and commitment (recall the checkered history of the Denver Airport baggage-handling system).[11] Though it wasn't easy:

> It took eight weeks to put the brakes on it . . . with a lot of analysis. Went back through the criteria that make a good project. This is where it got politically challenging. You want to be honest [about] how bad things are, but you don't want to focus on the people. The people are trying their hardest. You don't want them to feel bad. We built a lot of collateral around why we were red in so many places. We'd overstretched as a company, group, and team.
>
> What was more important than finding a scapegoat was doing a reset. Tried to separate the people from the

failure. . . . They were busting their butts, giving up holidays. Generally the team was doing what it was being asked.

Their Stop-Look-Listen practice gave them the ability to make an informed decision. Their understanding of the practice of mixing allowed them to consider, and then walk away from, alternatives to shutting down the project.

Next came a request to present at the worldwide IT managers' conference. Brett's boss said, "This is such an awesome example of success." Brett replied, "I just killed a $20 million project!" His boss said, "Get up in front of five hundred IT managers and tell the story of how you killed this thing." Five hundred more IT managers learned about Brett's plugged-in management approach through this practice of sharing.

Brett gave the presentation; he says his friends still laugh about it. Remember, this was early in Brett's career. The amount of support from management was critical. They said, "You never learn when things are going great."

And learn they did: "Ironically, a year later, after rebuilding their reputation, the same team went after the same problems—structured it right from the beginning. Focused on all of the lessons learned: starting off with change management, managing scope, exec support. Hugely successful. They will hearken back that those were some of the greatest days: on-time delivery, camaraderie, hitting stretch goals."

I asked Brett, "Given that your team could have fallen prey to escalation of commitment, what would you say made this one different?" He cited the aforementioned management support and the follow-on: "Ultimately jumping back into the same problem and solving it: having the right people, right roles, right player positions. . . . You may want so badly to solve problem X, the team may want to take it on, the business is there—but if you don't have the right people, stop until you do. . . . If you don't have an organizational change management plan, it really isn't the individual contributor's problem. If you haven't managed scope, it really isn't the individual contributor's problem."

The eContact story shows plugged-in management by all involved. It was a technology project with all the risks of technology projects everywhere: scope creep, complexity, and so on. What made their response plugged in was the clear understanding that the problems weren't about the technology. The problems were about the goals (organizational issues) and extreme motivation and commitment (people's responses to the goals). Killing the project required being able to see all three aspects (people, technology, organization) at once, perceiving that there was no hope, given the three aspects as they stood, and making a tough choice. Resurrecting the project also entailed plugged-in management. The basic technology goal was still sound. Managing the organization and people issues with the lessons learned from the first go-round tied the process together.

The eContact case shows how much more difficult it is to kill a project than to make the adoption decision—but when the killing is done well, it can demonstrate an example of plugged-in management. It's a story of how people and organization/management are tied to the heart of technology development, death, and resurrection.

How Did You Do?

These were incredibly complex situations, probably from outside your own industry. Check back on your self-assessment results at the end of Chapter Six, and feel confidence in your responses if you see yourself developing strength in a practice noted as needing development.

You may get continuing value from these situations, or others from your or your colleagues' experience, if you are able to see parallels in your own setting. The ability to refer back to a prior example gives you a head start on each of the practices of plugging in. The Stop-Look-Listen practice can be facilitated if you can use prior situations to help you identify options, quickly find data to support your decision making, or possibly apply feedback from prior situations to the current one. The mixing practice is greatly helped if you can see similarities among the stakeholders and so be better prepared to estimate their needs. Additionally, you may be able to extrapolate from one setting to the next around the different BUILDER topics introduced in Chapter Four. Finally, you are on the receiving end of sharing when you can learn from someone else's plugged-in management. Take advantage of this and then pass it on!

• •

Passing it on is what I'm going to do in Chapter Eight. I've been following a particular innovation for the last couple of years, and I want to share its unique characteristics as our main closing example.

chapter
EIGHT

The Layers of Plugged-In Management

This book is built on the examples set by the many plugged-in managers who let me tell their stories. I have one more story to tell. I saved this one for last, as it is a unique chance to see how an organization and its employees can thrive when they are plugged in. How does an *organization* practice plugged-in management? Through the implementation of plugged-in practices at all levels and functional areas of the organization that is. Just as plugged-in management is more powerful to the extent that ideas are shared with others (the third practice of a plugged-in manager—Chapter Five), plugged-in management is also more powerful when practiced inside an organization with plugged-in management practices mixed throughout the organization's policies and procedures. This last story highlights how a relatively young manager joined a plugged-in management company and learned to make the most of the opportunities.

The Brainstorm Story

Tad Milbourn is a twenty-something Silicon Valley success. But Tad is not your stereotypical Silicon Valley success story. Unlike Steve Jobs and Steve Wozniak of Apple, he finished college before starting work in Silicon Valley. Unlike Mark Zuckerberg of Facebook, Tad did not start a company in his college dorm. (Tad hasn't even founded his own company—yet!) And unlike Tony Hsieh, CEO of Zappos, Tad is not a multimillionaire with an iconic management style. Tad is a Silicon Valley success because he has added extreme value to a long-standing Silicon Valley company through his and his company's ability to plug in.

Immediately after graduating from college, Tad joined Intuit, the company that brings us Quicken, QuickBooks, and TurboTax. He had always been interested in science and technology, but in high school and college he developed an interest in why people do the things they do. Recall how many of our plugged-in examples have been similar cases: people interested in a wide breadth of issues who then have an insight that leads them to begin to mix people, technology, and organizational process together.

Tad moved to Mountain View, California, Intuit's headquarters city, but was quickly sent to Intuit's main call center in Tucson, Arizona, as part of the company's Rotational Development Program. Intuit mixed a batch of twelve new-hire business types and seven new-hire engineers together for three months of classroom training on products and time on the floor of the customer service call center.

"Generally, people start to silo quickly, but our group by nature was cross-functional," Tad said in a 2010 podcast describing the organizational process.[1] That was one of the dynamics that led to the group's members being able to innovate together.

Tad also talks about the value he gained from listening to the customers, the people. Chatting with a customer to pass the time while waiting for the customer's software to install taught him a lot about how the customers saw Intuit products and the context in which they use them. "Now when I see a report talking about units, it's not units. It's the woman outside of Philly where QuickBooks let her work from home and be with her family." He was able to see the human context as well as the technology.

When Tad and his colleagues got back to Mountain View, they dove into their jobs with great enthusiasm. They had been primed by their experience in Tucson and quickly began to think about how best to use their 10 percent "unstructured time."

A practice made famous by 3M and, more recently, Google and Intuit, unstructured time is organizational permission for individuals to work on projects of their own choosing. At Intuit, employees are offered 10 percent of their time; at Google, engineers are offered 20 percent; and at 3M, employees are offered 15 percent. The granting of unstructured time is official recognition that employees are a part of the innovation process, even if their jobs may not be formally part of research and development. There is generally flexibility around how the process works, and the time is scheduled around organizational demands.

Tad and the others started looking for ways they might pool their time and talent on some project. These new hires were plugged in. In the following section, I show how they took on each of the three practices of plugged-in management as they built a great tool and process.

First Practice: Stop-Look-Listen

Once a week, five of the new hires would get together to talk about their work. This simple process allowed them to *stop* and reflect on their opportunities and challenges.

They immediately identified how hard it was for them to find the information they needed to do their jobs. Their meetings quickly focused on what they might do to solve this problem for everyone at Intuit. They were *looking* for an existing solution to their problem, or ways to combine existing tools and practices in a way that would meet their needs. These new hires had gone through college using Google Search and Facebook to get great access to information and networks of support; unfortunately, these tools weren't useful for finding internal organization knowledge and support. The group saw this as an opportunity for innovation: Create a Google Search or Facebook tool for Intuit.

Tad recalls, "We started to push the idea at the company and found it more difficult than we thought it should be." Intuit had a process for contributing an innovation, but it was complicated and more appropriate for a formal organizational innovation process, not an emergent Google/Facebook–type innovation that would draw on the social network of the organization. Here the team was taking their initial idea and *listening* as they made various proposals. As the story continues, notice that listening remains an important part of their process.

The more the new hires thought about the hurdles they were encountering in proposing their own ideas, the more they began to see that instead of creating a broad Google/Facebook tool, they should probably build a tool to support innovation contributions. This was the beginning of Intuit Brainstorm.

Second Practice: Mixing

Over the following weekend, the most technically sophisticated member of the team put together the basics of the Brainstorm web application. The team's goal was to reduce the barriers to contributing and participating in innovation. They used a simple technology design—if you have an idea, push this button; if you want to discover others' ideas, push that button—coupled with an understanding of the organization's unstructured time for motivation and an understanding of their colleagues' human desire for a process that would not get in the way of their creativity. They *mixed* together a design that effectively used human capabilities, technology tools, and organizational process.

People

The new hires predicted, correctly, that simple tools could harness the energy employees had for their unstructured time. Intuit understood that people, even without direction, are the source of great ideas.

Organizational Processes

Intuit had gone out of its way to recruit forward-looking new hires and to give them a solid common background on the company through the rotational program. In addition, the company had set the stage for success with their organizational practice of 10 percent unstructured time, which Tad and the new hires were happy to take advantage of to build a new tool for the company.

Technology Tools

The new hires understood how social media technologies like internet chat, collaboration spaces, profiles, and an internet-based search engine could be a benefit in a global company. They understood that their company did not have the tools for them to easily share or grow ideas. They also understood that the available formal innovation system couldn't handle fragile emergent ideas because the user needed to be ready with a full business plan to make that process work.

From that first weekend, they had a start. Brainstorm evolved from an initial pain point to a place where innovators could capture and grow an idea through collaboration.

Third Practice: Sharing

The team incorporated *sharing* right into the design of the tool, and as a result the use of the Brainstorm process went viral. Brainstorm's features evolved to include the ability to email people about ideas. Something like, "Hey, I saw this idea on Brainstorm and thought you might be interested." An email that started out as focused on the innovation idea then also turned into internal marketing for the Brainstorm process itself.

Sharing is built into the tool and into the organizational practices that have evolved to support the ideas growing within the tool. Meetings are held to discuss ideas that have developed to a stage where they need formal organizational support. Senior managers come together and work with the innovation teams to suggest tests (listening) with customers that will help the innovation team get feedback before taking the next step. Intuit's resources include a website where customers can volunteer to evaluate new ideas—a combination of human interest, technology tools, and organizational processes. Plugged-in management is modeled at each stage.

In the Long Run . . .

How were these relatively inexperienced new hires successful at making such a significant contribution inside a well-established organization? Tad and the other new hires mixed available technology tools and organizational practices and policies into a powerful structure in which the people of their organization can succeed. They practiced plugged-in management. Being plugged in gives you the vision to see choices across each dimension of people, technology tools, and organizational process—and the wisdom to mix them together into new and powerful organizational approaches.

Tad became the product manager for Brainstorm. In the second year after the rotational program, Intuit gave Tad a Scott Cook Innovation Award, named for Intuit's founder. In less than three years, Brainstorm had been rolled out to more than twenty external customers and was serving as a resource to the majority of Intuit employees. As of this writing, over six hundred thousand people have access to Brainstorm, and Intuit credits new products like ViewMyPaycheck.com to the Brainstorm effect.

Tad's success had nothing to do with the dot-com world of Silicon Valley and everything to do with how Tad and Intuit think about leadership and innovation. His achievement came about through the melding of his and his colleagues' plugged-in management skills with the plugged-in nature of Intuit's organizational design.

Tad was hired into an organization that was primed to make use of his plugged-in management skills. Some other organizations might have fought against Tad and his peers' new ideas; Intuit gave them access to technology tools, provided an organizational process that gave them time and permission to come up with new ideas, and created an environment in which people are willing and able to work together around innovation. Plugged-in management was layered into each level of the organization. Tad and the others are members of the Facebook generation, to be sure, but more important than their technical skills was their ability to see how the tools of this generation could be applied within an existing organizational system. They knew how to blend their understanding of their fellow employees, technology tools, and organizational practice into a real-world value. Mixed together, the Brainstorm process and Intuit's generally innovative approach are more powerful than any single hiring decision, technology tool, or organizational practice could be on its own.

The Brainstorm tool continues to evolve. For example, the Brainstorm team added a Challenges feature that allows leaders to focus innovators on pressing strategic issues.

Intuit itself has also evolved. Brainstorm is now a formal part of Intuit's ongoing process for supporting innovation in the organization. Managers of different areas and product lines routinely track projects on Brainstorm and call meetings as they see ideas progress. Innovation is treated gently. These are not "grill" sessions, as they might be at other organizations. The ideas are understood to be young and open to improvement. Rather than creating high hurdles across a wide variety of requirements, managers ask the idea teams what the next step will be, to enable a judgment call about the viability of the idea.

Test phases often involve a quick connection to customers through the easy-to-use Intuit Labs, which provides a public Internet sandbox (website) where interested customers can interact with Intuit ideas at early stages and where Intuit innovators can get quick feedback from the real world.[2] Again, plugged-in management has led Intuit and the innovators to build a people/technology/organizational platform that helps everyone with new ideas.

This story represents the *layered* method of plugging-in—the strongest kind. The individuals *and* the organization see the importance of mixing together the people, technology tools, and organizational process. Tad's broad background has led him, like many of the people described earlier, to practice plugged-in management. Intuit leadership has gone back to its innovative beginnings and created a technology infrastructure that can support new organizational policies and employees in its innovative practice.

Plugging In as a Life Skill

Although many of the examples I've given were related to big organizational events, plugged-in management is more than a strategy for big organizational change. Plugging in is a life skill that we all need, all the time. Plugging in is valuable for our daily decisions concerning:

- Whether or not to take a laptop to your next meeting
- Whether or not to have the meeting
- The style of presentation to use with a new client
- How to keep virtual and not-so-virtual teams on track

- Whether to email a colleague, walk down the hall to the colleague's office, or both
- How to get in front of the curve with your company's strategies for new ways of interacting with customers, employees, and the world

You need to mix human capability, technology tools, and organizational processes together to be effective in today's environment—and, frankly, in *every* environment that has existed since humans have had tools such as sticks, stone axes, and fire (which presented early humans with a need for the division of labor).[3] Any approach that doesn't consider all three dimensions—technology, organization, and people—and effectively balance them will miss out on value. One of my favorite examples of this was presented in Chapter Five: the bank loan group that started with a multimillion-dollar technology implementation but ended with the group sticking with older technology and taking on an organizational process change designed by the employees who had originally been seen as the base of the problem!

The ability to acknowledge the possibilities across the dimensions of people, technology, and organizations and then to mix them into strong and dynamic organizational strategies and methods is what distinguishes people with the ability to plug in from those without it. Plugged-in management may be the most powerful skill we have in modern organizations. Plugging in allows us to see our opportunities and make effective decisions about basic work process, technology, and organizational design. The people involved change, technologies change, and organizational needs change. Your organizational design and management approach should change, or at least be reevaluated, in sync with those changes.

The answer isn't always to take on the new technology or the latest organizational methods. Plugged-in management provides a method for making the decision as well as any supporting changes that may be required as a result of the decision. There are times to integrate sophisticated technologies and times to stick with a tech-light method. For example, learning may be supported with the metrics and video capability provided by internet-based testing—or using a such a technology may be a detriment to those less experienced in using the Internet.[4] We need to make informed decisions about the best path.

Consider telecommuting (the ability to work from home or another location away from the normal workplace). Many organizations offer telecommuting options to support work-life balance, reduce pollution due to commuting, or just provide increased flexibility. As is true of most complex organizational choices, there are costs and benefits. The work-life balance goal can be met by allowing employees to spend the majority of their time away from the office—but there is a cost in terms of relationships at work.[5] Plugged-in employees and managers will be more likely to find a way to balance these effects. For example, the organization could move to a workweek with core days where everyone is expected to work at the office so that face-to-face interactions are more easily managed.

There are organizational realities that may enhance or inhibit the use of a particular technology or practice—organizations have policies about the use of technologies within their walls and vary in levels of support and availability of network access they provide to guests. Just as you should think about what to take on a trip, you should think about what to take into different technology or organization environments. I'm recalling a first-time presenter arriving at a conference to give a pitch and being told that the company did not allow individual laptops to be connected to the projectors. He then had to scramble for a way to get the presentation file onto the provided computer. If this first-timer had been more plugged in, he might have either anticipated the need for a thumb drive or thought to email the presentation to the organizers in advance.

Become Wise in the Ways of Plugging In

Like other forms of practical intelligence, the ability to plug in can be developed in a variety of ways: through broad work experience, reflecting on how challenges were overcome, working with plugged-in mentors, or reading a book like this one, filled with vivid, real-world examples.[6] The ability to plug in is a kind of wisdom. This means that plugging in is more than knowing facts; the focus is on finding solutions that are prudent in a given situation and not swayed by passion or shallow thinking.[7] Plugged-in management is a vaccination against technology and management fads.

Look for opportunities that can trigger plugged-in management for both you and your organization. Consider Suzanne Kirkpatrick. Her past roles include program manager, Office of the Chief Software Architect at Microsoft and executive committee program coordinator for Strong Angel III, a large international disaster-response demonstration.[8] She says her epiphany regarding the need to mix all three plugged-in dimensions together at once came during Strong Angel III. She had extensive experience in cross-boundary collaboration in politically complex and technologically challenged environments. She spent a year living in Kabul, Afghanistan, with the United Nations Development Programme building public-private technology partnerships. In her work both with the United Nations and in an earlier position at Cisco Systems, she developed information technology capacity and information-sharing systems for people, governments, and organizations in developing countries; programs to support women in technology; and methods to link local communities to national and international development initiatives. Yet Suzanne says it was during Strong Angel III (she was the informatics coordinator) that the need—indeed, the demand—to manage people, technology, and organization as part of a combined equation became explicit in her thinking.

In Strong Angel III, they had all the communications gear, Wi-Fi networks, geographic information systems modeling, data encryption, and so on, and the most brilliant technical minds— but it soon became clear that technology alone would not be able to support effective cooperation in response to a real large-scale disaster. They had formal agreements, memoranda of under- standing across the many major and smaller organizations—but organization alone couldn't do it. They had the social network piece, personal relationships, and community-building efforts— but again, that alone couldn't support the need. Suzanne notes that filling the "interesting space in between" is what brought the teams together to be successful.

Her work at Microsoft reinforced her belief that it's the space in between that matters (in my words, how the people, technol- ogy, and organization dimensions are mixed together). Her research and support of the company's distributed development teams helped her see that "each case, each team, it's always a reconfirmation . . . the space in between, the gaps in the middle of those three things." Where there are gaps, they try to make the links.

Some people may be better or worse at seeing and managing these gaps. Suzanne thinks both organizational and individual opportunities make a difference. If an organization "sets up a culture that encourages [managing the connections across tech- nology, organization, people], you might see more of that coming to the surface, being more conscious and intentional about that framework and operating in that framework. A lot of organiza- tions understand the importance of one or two of the three aspects [people, technology, organization], and the other(s) are overlooked." From the individual perspective, she thinks that people "who have had a breadth of personal experience across different kinds of organizations, people, and cultures (versus staying within the software development function, or staying in one country)" could be more likely to see possibilities to plug in and mix the dimensions together. This breadth of experience in working with complex systems "could expose them to important underlying currents."

Not Your Grandmother's World

I once heard technology-and-work thought leader Steve Barley[9] say in a keynote speech that his grandmother lived in times of greater technology upheaval than we do.[10] I've given this comment a lot of thought over the years, yet I've never been able to see it his way. People in our grandmothers' time had travelled in everything from a covered wagon to a jet plane and transitioned from farming to office and factory work. These changes did require dramatic adjustments, but they were also discrete and noticeable. Today's changes may be more subtle, but also come much more quickly. Anne Rutkowski and Carol Saunders argue that the information overload that many of us feel isn't just about having more information to deal with.[11] The emotional and cognitive overload we feel also comes from trying to manipulate all this information—in the context of having to forget old ways of receiving and processing information—more frequently than in the past.

Plugged-in managers find ways to manage this deluge. Plugged-in managers see the technical and organizational opportunities and the organizational and human costs it will take to mix them together. Through this process they are better able to decide when to take on a change and when to wait for the next wave.

• •

I haven't tried to write a cookbook with specific ingredients and steps for plugged-in management, because each set of stakeholders, technology, and organization will create a different environment. Just as each dish your favorite chef makes is unique, your own application of plugged-in management also needs to be unique and designed for your particular setting. Plugged-in managers are those who are able to react to, adapt, and grow with our rapidly changing technological environment. It is the plugged-in managers who will have the most success in this changing world.

NOTES

Chapter 1. Plugging In to the Twenty-First Century

1. Here we talk about managers' ability to plug in. In academic circles we call this "systems savvy." Griffith, T. L., McGrath, R. E., & Poole, M. S. (2011). Systems savvy and organizational memory. Presented at the 17th Organization Science Winter Conference, Steamboat Springs, CO.
2. Van de Ven, A. H., & Drazin, R. (1985). The concept of fit in contingency theory. In B. M. Staw & L. L. Cummings (Eds.), *Research in Organizational Behavior* (Vol. 7, pp. 333–365). Greenwich, CT: JAI Press.
3. Brooks, F. P., Jr. (1986). No silver bullet—Essence and accident in software engineering. In H.-J. Kugler, ed., *Proceedings of the IFIP Tenth World Computing Conference,* Elsevier Science B. V., Amsterdam, NL, pp. 1069–1076.
4. Trist, E. L., & Bamforth, K. W. (1951). Some social and psychological consequences of the long-wall method of coal-getting. *Human Relations, 4,* 3–38.

Chapter 2. Why You Need Plugged-In Management

1. MacIver, K. (2010, August 4). Google chief Eric Schmidt on the data explosion. Retrieved on 7/14/11 from http://www.i-cio.com/blog/august-2010/eric-schmidt-exabytes-of-data
2. King, R. (2008). How cloud computing is changing the world. *BusinessWeek.* Retrieved on 7/14/11 from http://www.businessweek.com/technology/content/aug2008/tc2008082_445669.htm
3. Wim Elfrink discusses globalization and the decision by Cisco Systems Inc. to focus on India. (2007). News@Cisco. Retrieved on

7/14/11 from http://newsroom.cisco.com/dlls/2007/ts_071207 .html

4. Zeidner, R. (2010). Heady debate: Rely on temps or hire staff? *Society for Human Resource Management.* Retrieved on 7/14/11 from http://www.shrm.org/Publications/hrmagazine/EditorialContent/2010/0210/Pages/0210zeidner.aspx

5. Li, C. (2010). *Open leadership: How social technology can transform the way you lead.* San Francisco: Jossey-Bass.

6. Roth, D. (2009). The answer factory: Demand media and the fast, disposable, and profitable as hell media model. *Wired Magazine.* Retrieved on 7/14/11 from http://www.wired.com/magazine/2009/10/ff_demandmedia/all/1

7. Zittrain, J. (Producer). (2009). Minds for sale. Podcast retrieved on 2/17/11 from http://www.youtube.com/watch?v=Dw3h-rae3uo

8. Zittrain, J. (2008). *The future of the Internet—And how to stop it.* New Haven, CT: Yale University Press.

9. IBM announces new software, vision for community driven development. (2007). Retrieved on 7/14/11 from http://www.redorbit.com/news/technology/963311/ibm_announces_new_software_vision_for_community_driven_development/index.html

10. Tapscott, D. (2008). *Grown up digital: How the Net generation is changing your world.* New York: McGraw-Hill, p. 18.

11. Palfrey, J., & Gasser, U. (2008). *Born digital: Understanding the first generation of digital natives.* New York: Basic Books, p. 1.

12. Tapscott, *Grown up digital.*

13. Hagel, J., Brown, J. S., & Davison, L. (2010). *The power of pull: How small moves, smartly made, can set big things in motion.* New York: Basic Books.

14. Tapscott, D., & Ticoll, D. (2003). *The naked corporation: How the age of transparency will revolutionize business.* New York: Free Press.

15. Tapscott, D., & Williams, A. D. (2010). *Macrowikinomics: Rebooting business and the world.* New York: Portfolio Hardcover.

16. Ibid., p. 28.

17. Mayfield, R. (Producer). (2009). We're shifting from a need-to-know to a need-to-share culture. Ideas Project. Podcast retrieved on 2/17/2011 from http://www.ideasproject.com/idea_person.webui?id=4414#

18. Hsieh, T. (2010). *Delivering happiness: A path to profits, passion, and purpose.* New York: Business Plus.

19. Disney Institute: Our story. Retrieved on 2/22/2011 from http://disneyinstitute.com/about_us/our_story.aspx

20. Bennis, W., Goleman, D., & O'Toole, J. (2008). *Transparency: How leaders create a culture of candor.* San Francisco: Jossey-Bass.

21. Merchant, N. (2010). *The new how: Creating business solutions through collaborative strategy*. Sebastopol, CA: O'Reilly Media.
22. Ibid.
23. Ibid.
24. Stack, J., & Burlingham, B. (1992). *The great game of business: The only sensible way to run a company*. New York: Doubleday/Currency.
25. Bennis, Goleman, & O'Toole, *Transparency*, p. 109.
26. Anderson, C. (2010). In the next industrial revolution, atoms are the new bits. *Wired Magazine*. Retrieved on 3/7/2011 from http://www.wired.com/magazine/2010/01/ff_newrevolution/
27. BuildItWith.Me. Retrieved on 2/22/2011 from http://builditwith.me/
28. Von Hippel, E. (2006). *Democratizing innovation*. Cambridge, MA: MIT Press, p. 118.
29. See, for example, Watkins, M. (2003). *The first 90 days: Critical success strategies for new leaders at all levels*. Cambridge, MA: Harvard Business Press, p. 45.
30. A blog is a "web log," written by an individual or a group. Blogs may be diaries, lab notebooks, or running commentary.
31. Bennis, Goleman, & O'Toole, *Transparency*.

Part One. The Three Practices of the Plugged-In Manager

1. You can sign up for a free tour at http://www.zapposinsights.com/main/experiences/tours/.
2. Fortune 100 best companies to work for (2010). Retrieved on 2/24/2011, from http://money.cnn.com/magazines/fortune/bestcompanies/2010/full_list/
3. Stambar, Z. (2010, February 24). Zappos' customer service draws raves in a new report. Retrieved on 7/14/11 from http://www.internetretailer.com/2010/03/22/zappos-customer-service-draws-raves-in-a-new-report
4. For part of the story, see Hsieh, T. (2010). *Delivering happiness: The path to profits, passion and purpose*. New York: Business Plus, pp. 108–109.
5. Personal correspondence with Keith Glynn. Many thanks to Amelia Smith and the "Ask Anything" team at Zappos Insights for connecting us.
6. Marks, M. E., Lee, H. L., & Hoyt, D. (2009). Zappos.com: Developing a supply chain to deliver WOW! Retrieved on 7/14/11 from https://gsbapps.stanford.edu/cases/detail1.asp?Document_ID=3200
7. Keith's quotes are copyright © 2010 Zappos.com, Inc., or its affiliates.

8. Hsieh, *Delivering happiness*, p. 116.
9. Ibid., p. 118.
10. Ibid., pp. 118–119.
11. Nevins, A. (Producer). (2009). Institute of Business Forecasting, Demand Planning and Forecasting: Best Practices Conference. Slideshare retrieved on 2/24/11 from http://www.slideshare.net/constancekorol/zapposibfdpfc2009
12. Hsieh, *Delivering happiness*, p. xi.
13. Zappos Insights: About. (2011). Retrieved on 2/24/2011 from http://www.zapposinsights.com/main/about/

Chapter 3. First Practice: Stop-Look-Listen

1. Dan Schultz, phone interview and personal correspondence with the author, November 2009.
2. See, for example, Weick, K. E. (1984). Small wins: Redefining the scale of social problems. *American Psychologist, 39*, 40–49.
3. Clark, G. (2007). Exactly what about Six Sigma doesn't work. Retrieved on 4/29/2011 from http://www.isixsigma.com/index.php?option=com_k2&view=item&id=3653
4. Fiol, C. M., & O'Connor, E. J. (2003). Waking up! Mindfulness in the face of bandwagons. *Academy of Management Review, 28*, 54–70.
5. Corporate Information: About Google. (2011). Retrieved on 2/24/2011 from http://www.google.com/corporate/
6. Mayer, M. (Producer). (2009). Innovation at Google: The physics of data. Podcast retrieved on 2/24/2011 from http://www.parc.com/event/936/innovation-at-google.html
7. Darling, M., Parry, C., & Moore, J. (2005). Learning in the thick of it. *Harvard Business Review, 83*(7), 84–92.
8. Dixon, N. M., Allen, N., Burgess, T., Kilner, P., & Schweitzer, S. (2005). *CompanyCommand: Unleashing the power of the Army profession.* West Point, NY: Center for the Advancement of Leader Development & Organizational Learning.
9. Le Meur, L. (Producer). (2008). Sharing changes everything. Podcast retrieved on 2/24/2011 from http://www.ideasproject.com/idea_person.webui?id=528—quoted material begins at 2:10.
10. Chesbrough, H. W. (2003). *Open innovation: The new imperative for creating and profiting from technology.* Boston: Harvard Business School Publishing.
11. IDEO Labs: About. Retrieved on 2/24/2011 from http://labs.ideo.com/about/

12. Google Labs. Retrieved on 2/24/2011 from http://www.googlelabs .com/
13. PARC Living Laboratory. Retrieved on 2/24/2011 from http://www .parc.com/work/demos-tools.html
14. NASA Innovation Incubator. Retrieved on 2/24/2011 from http:// www.nasa.gov/offices/ipp/innovation_incubator/index.html
15. LotusLive Lab. Retrieved on 2/24/2011 from https://www.lotuslive .com/en/lotuslive_labs
16. MyStarbucks Idea. Retrieved on 2/24/2011 from http:// mystarbucksidea.force.com/ideaHome
17. Kalil, T. (2010). Grand challenges of the 21st century. Retrieved on 2/24/2011 from http://www.whitehouse.gov/blog/2010/02/04/ grand-challenges-21st-century
18. Chesbrough, H. W., & Teece, D. J. (1996). When is virtual virtuous? Organizing for innovation. *Harvard Business Review, 74*(1), 65–73.
19. Ochman, B. L. (2009). Three top ways to damage your brand with social media. Retrieved on 2/24/11 from http://www.whatsnextblog .com/archives/2009/10/three_top_ways_to_damage_your_brand _with_social_media.asp
20. Reisner, R. (2009). Comcast's Twitter man. Retrieved on 7/14/11 from http://www.businessweek.com/managing/content/jan2009/ ca20090113_373506.htm
21. Comments section of Ochman, B. L. (2009). Three top ways to damage your brand with social media. Retrieved on 4/25/2011 from http://socialmediatoday.com/index.php?q=SMC/127073
22. Arnst, C. (2010). Hospitals: Radical cost surgery. *Bloomberg Business-week*. Retrieved on 7/14/11 from http://www.businessweek.com/ magazine/content/10_03/b4163040943750.htm. Kim Williams, the chief nursing officer at Providence Regional, was kind enough to walk me through their process. Judy Espedal, a Cardiac Critical Care staff nurse, then gave me the history, and Dr. Jim Brevig, director of cardiac surgery, the context.
23. Brown, K. K., & Gallant, D. (2006). Impacting patient outcomes through design: Acuity adaptable care/universal room design. *Critical Care Nursing Quarterly, 29*(4), 326–341.
24. Starbuck, W. H., & Milliken, F. J. (1988). Executives' perceptual filters: What they notice and how they make sense. In D. C. Hambrick (Ed.), *The executive effect: Concepts and methods for studying top managers.* Greenwich, CT: JAI Press.
25. Brevig, J., McDonald, J., Zelinka, E. S., Gallagher, T., Jin, R., & Grunkemeier, G. L. (2009). Blood transfusion reduction in cardiac

surgery: Multidisciplinary approach at a community hospital. *The Annals of Thoracic Surgery, 87*(2), 532–540.

26. The team used statistical process control as an observational technique. Whether formally or informally applied, statistical process control is a method of routinely tracking outcome data with control limits for what should be considered normal and how to recognize trends moving out of this normal band of outcomes.

27. Salancik, G. R. (1977). Commitment and the control of organizational behavior and belief. In B. M. Staw & G. R. Salancik (Eds.), *New directions in organizational behavior.* Chicago, IL: St. Clair Press.

Chapter 4. Second Practice: Mixing

1. See also Allison Rossett's discussion of silver bullets and systems solutions. Rossett, A. (2009). *First things fast* (2nd ed.). San Francisco: Pfeiffer.

2. Fisher and Ury's classic book *Getting to Yes* provides great background on how to negotiate. For a more advanced view, I suggest *Negotiating Rationally* by Bazerman and Neale. Fisher, R., & Ury, W. (1981). *Getting to yes.* Boston, MA: Houghton Mifflin; Bazerman, M. H., & Neale, M. A. (1992). *Negotiating rationally.* New York/Toronto: Free Press.

3. Salancik, G. R. (1977). Commitment and the control of organizational behavior and belief. In B. M. Staw & G. R. Salancik (Eds.), *New directions in organizational behavior.* Chicago, IL: St. Clair Press.

4. Research suggests there is value to the range of knowledge covered by a network. The more breadth of knowledge held by the members of the network (in this instance, the knowledge held by the initial set of people who can access the wiki), the greater the value to the organization's knowledge management. See Reagans, R., & McEvily (2003). Network structure and knowledge transfer: The effects of cohesion and range. *Administrative Science Quarterly, 48,* 240–267. Many knowledge management experts are also turning away from the idea of pilot programs (smaller initial membership groups). See, for example, McAfee, A. (2010). No more pilots. Retrieved on 3/10/2011 from http://andrewmcafee.org/2010/04/drop-the-pilot/; and the follow-up post, McAfee, A. (2010). Drop the pilot, part 2. Retrieved on 3/10/2011 from http://andrewmcafee.org/2010/05/drop-the-pilot-part-2/

5. Flinn, R. (2010). Sephora, Best Buy enlist social-media consultants to attract "super users." *Bloomberg.* Retrieved on 7/14/11 from

http://www.bloomberg.com/news/2010–12–09/sephora-best-buy
-snag-super-users-with-social-media-tools.html

6. Bazerman, M. H., & Neale, M. A. (1992). *Negotiating rationally*. New York: Free Press, pp. 74–75.

7. Issue-by-issue negotiations are more likely to result in compromises that leave the stakeholders worse off than if they had considered mixing the issues and looking for trade-offs. Thompson, L. L., Mannix, E. A., & Bazerman, M. H. (1989). Group negotiation: Effects of decision rule, agenda, and aspiration. *Journal of Personality and Social Psychology, 54*, 86–95.

8. Hoffer, J. A., George, J. F., & Valacich, J. S. (2008). *Modern systems analysis and design* (5th ed.). Upper Saddle River, NJ: Pearson Prentice Hall.

9. Moreland, R. L., Argote, L., & Krishnan, R. (1998). Training people to work in groups. In R. S. Tindale, L. Heath, J. Edwards, E. J. Posvoc, F. B. Bryant, Y. Suarez-Balcazar, E. Henderson-King, & J. Myers (Eds.), *Applications of theory and research on groups to social issues* (Vol. 4, pp. 37–60). New York: Plenum.

10. Thank you to Al Lindahl for giving me a basic understanding of the culinary process.

11. Mogil, H. M. (2009). Southwest Airlines Boarding Process. Retrieved on 4/26/2011 from http://www.associatedcontent.com/article/1682572/southwest_airlines_boarding_process_pg3.html. The Southwest Airlines corporate blog provides a variety of positive and negative observations about the change: Stevens, B. (2008). New boarding process—After the holidays. Retrieved on 2/24/2011 from http://www.blogsouthwest.com/2008/01/14/new-boarding-process-after-the-holidays/

12. See p. 39 of the April 2011 Department of Transportation Air Travel Consumer Report. Southwest Airlines has the lowest ratio of complaints per passengers boarded of all major U.S. carriers and second overall (the regional Mesa Airlines placed first in this report). Retrieved on 7/14/11 from http://airconsumer.dot.gov/reports/2011/April/2011AprilATCR.pdf

13. Louis, M. R., & Sutton, R. I. (1991). Switching cognitive gears: From habits of mind to active thinking. *Human Relations, 44*(1), 55–76.

Chapter 5. Third Practice: Sharing

1. For example, see Flores-Pereira, M. T., Davel, E., & Cavedone, N. R. (2008). Drinking beer and understanding organizational culture embodiment. *Human Relations, 61*(7), 1007–1026.

2. Schein, E. H. (1993). On dialogue, culture, and organizational learning. *Organizational Dynamics, 22,* 40–51.
3. Kouzes, J. M., & Posner, B. Z. (2007). *The leadership challenge* (4th ed.). San Francisco: Jossey-Bass, p. 340.
4. Kouzes, J. M., & Posner, B. Z. (1995). An instructor's guide to *The leadership challenge.* Retrieved on 7/15/11 from http://media.wiley.com/assets/57/11/lc_jb_instructors_guide.pdf
5. Saffer, D. (2007). Design schools: Please start teaching design again. Retrieved on 2/24/2011 from http://www.adaptivepath.com/blog/2007/03/06/design-schools-please-start-teaching-design-again/
6. Mader, S. (2007). *Wikipatterns.* New York: Wiley.
7. Quotations not attributed to Stewart Mader's book are from our interview of May 17, 2010, San Francisco.
8. Mader, *Wikipatterns,* p. 31.
9. I interviewed the Nucor managers quoted in this chapter in August 2010.
10. If you access your email through your web browser (Gmail and Yahoo! Mail are examples), you are using the cloud to store your email. Many companies are moving their (and your!) data to the cloud, where updates, backups, and access can be more flexible than if this information were stored locally on your hard drive.
11. Kepes, B. (2010). Change the system, not the technology. Retrieved on 2/24/2011 from http://diversity.net.nz/change-the-system-not-the-technology/2010/04/17/
12. Ben Kepes interview with the author, April 16, 2010, San Francisco.
13. Moreland, R. L., & Myaskovsky, L. (2000). Explaining the performance benefits of group training: Transactive memory or improved communication? *Organizational Behavior and Human Decision Processes, 82*(1), 117–133.
14. I had the pleasure of connecting with Jennifer after Queen Mavor, a colleague from a past Cisco project, emailed me with a list of people she sees as being plugged in (plugged-in managers can spot one another a mile away). Jennifer was working for WebEx, the Internet conferencing company, when WebEx was acquired by Cisco. She'd recently returned to consulting when I was able to catch up with her for a phone interview and email in January 2010.
15. Merchant, N. (2010). *The new how: Creating business solutions through collaborative strategy.* San Francisco: O'Reilly Media, p. 59.
16. Yoon, L. (2009). Tales of a sporting CIO. Retrieved on 2/24/2011 from http://www.ciozone.com/index.php/Career/Tales-of-a-Sporting-CIO.html

17. Rhonda Winter phone interview and personal correspondence with the author, April 2010.
18. Cross, J. (2006). *Informal learning: Rediscovering the natural pathways that inspire innovation and performance.* San Francisco: Pfeiffer, p. 16.
19. Even Facebook interactions can have learning value: If my students who access Facebook during class are checking with their friends about additional relevant examples, they may still be adding value to their overall learning. The class as a whole can even benefit if the student then shares those examples with the rest of us.
20. Cross, J. (2005). A great day. Retrieved on 4/27/2011 from http://www.internettime.com/2005/05/a-great-day/
21. Cross, *Informal learning*, p. iii.
22. Cross, J. (2003). Informal learning—the other 80%. Retrieved on 2/24/2011 from http://www.internettime.com/Learning/The%20Other%2080%25.htm
23. Adapted from Cocheu, T., & Griffith, T. L. (2008). Formal & informal learning. Figure retrieved on 7/15/11 from http://www.terrigriffith.com/blog/wp-content/uploads/2008/08/informlrn.jpg
24. An April 12, 2011 check of the Wikipedia entry turns up this new, unattributed discussion: ". . . the Chinese language origin of the phrase, if it exists, has not been found, making its authenticity, at least in its present form, very doubtful. One theory is that it may be related to the Chinese proverb translated as 'It's better to be a dog in a peaceful time than be a man in a chaotic period.'" Retrieved on 4/12/11 from http://en.wikipedia.org/wiki/May_you_live_in_interesting_times

Part Two. Learning to Plug In

1. Wolf Cramer is a past student and now guest speaker in my classes and public panels; he gave me some excellent insights on the real-world implications of developing a plugged-in practice. In the years since Wolf completed my executive MBA course, "Managing Innovation and Change," he has provided valuable comments on my blog and has had the opportunity to see and contribute to these ideas' evolution.

Chapter 6. Assess Your Ability to Plug In

1. You can also answer online at www.ThePluggedInManager.com. Answering online offers two benefits: The site will automatically plot

your feedback, and you won't give away your answers when you share this book—which I hope you will.

2. For example, the highly regulated financial industry has to tread carefully when it comes to communications with their customers; see "SEC scrutinises social media; Finra to re-examine guidance." (2011). Retrieved on 2/24/2011 from http://www.finextra.com/News/Fullstory.aspx?newsitemid=22276

3. Orasanu, J., & Connolly, T. (1997). The reinvention of decision making. In C. E. Zsambok & G. Klein (Eds.), *Naturalistic decision making* (pp. 3–22). Mahwah, NJ: Lawrence Erlbaum Associates.

4. Hollingshead, A. B. (1996). Information suppression and status persistence in group decision making: The effects of communication media. *Human Communication Research, 23*(2), 193–219.

Chapter 7. Plugging In Through Practice

1. Nadler, D., & Tushman, M. L. (1997). *Competing by design: The power of organizational architecture.* New York: Oxford University Press.

2. Amazon.com. (2010). Kindle (latest generation) license agreement and terms of use. Retrieved on 3/5/2011 from http://www.amazon.com/gp/help/customer/display.html?nodeId=200505590

3. Claburn, T. (2009). Amazon settles Kindle deletion lawsuit for $150,000. *InformationWeek.* Retrieved on 7/15/11 from http://www.informationweek.com/news/internet/ebusiness/showArticle.jhtml?articleID=220300915

4. Stone, B. (2009, July 17). Amazon erases Orwell books from Kindle. *New York Times.* Retrieved on 7/15/11 from http://www.nytimes.com/2009/07/18/technology/companies/18amazon.html?_r=2

5. Nucor. (2011). Our story. Retrieved on 3/1/2011 from http://nucor.com/story/chapter3/

6. Ibid.

7. Iverson, K. (1997). *Plain talk: Lessons from a business maverick.* New York: Wiley.

8. Thanks to David Hanson for the initial introduction to Nucor and the company background.

9. Dirk Petersen's Green Sheet letter to employees, August 2010.

10. Festinger, L., Schachter, S., & Back, K. W. (1950). *Social pressures in informal groups: A study of human factors in housing.* New York: Harper Brothers. This is the classic reference for the effects of location. Current discussions are available from: Armstrong, D. J., & Cole, P. (2002). Managing distances and differences in geographically dis-

tributed work groups. In P. Hinds & S. Kiesler (Eds.), *Distributed work.*
Cambridge, MA: MIT Press; Hinds, P., & Bailey, D. (2003). Out of
sight, out of sync: Understanding conflict in distributed teams.
Organization Science, 14, 615–632.

11. Montealegre, R., & Keil, M. (2000). De-escalating information technology projects: Lessons from the Denver International Airport.
Management Information Systems Quarterly, 24(3), 417–447.

Chapter 8. The Layers of Plugged-In Management

1. Pay Attention! Live life actively with Tad Milbourn—Episode no. 4.
(2010). Podcast retrieved on 3/2/2011 from http://innovatorsmix
.com/podcasts/pay-attention-live-life-actively-with-tad-milbourn/
2. Intuit Labs. Retrieved on 3/2/2011 from https://intuitlabs.com/
3. Smith, V. L. (1992). Economic principles in the emergence of
humankind: Presidential address to the Western Economic
Association. *Economic Inquiry, 30*(1), 1–13.
4. Naglieri, J. A., Drasgow, F., Schmit, M., Handler, L., Prifitera, A.,
Margolis, A., et al. (2004). Psychological testing on the Internet:
New problems, old issues. *American Psychologist, 59*(3), 150–162.
5. Gajendran, R. S., & Harrison, D. A. (2007). The good, the bad, and
the unknown about telecommuting: Meta-analysis of psychological
mediators and individual consequences. *Journal of Applied Psychology,
92*(6), 1524–1541.
6. Sternberg, R. J. (2000). *Practical intelligence in everyday life.* New York:
Cambridge University Press.
7. Sternberg, R. J. (Ed.). (1990). *Wisdom: Its nature, origins, and development.* New York: Cambridge University Press; and Jowett, B. (1942).
The dialogues of Plato. New York: Random House.
8. Strong Angel III was an international disaster-response demonstration attended by over eight hundred practitioners from more than
two hundred organizations across the public and private sectors,
government, nongovernmental organizations, and universities. For
more information, please see http://strongangel3.net/
9. Steve's classic piece is foundational to much of my thinking
about how people, organization, and technology interact.
Barley, S. R. (1986). Technology as an occasion for structuring:
Evidence from observations of CT scanners and the social order of
radiology departments. *Administrative Science Quarterly, 31*(1),
78–108.
10. Richard Florida and my colleague Alexander Field would agree with
Steve, but their analysis is focused on the national productivity

changes seen from 1929 to 1941, not a perception of our work. Field, A. (2006). Technological change and U.S. productivity growth in the interwar years. *Journal of Economic History*, *66*(1), 203–236; Florida, R. L. (2010). *The great reset: How new ways of living and working drive post-crash prosperity*. New York: HarperCollins.

11. Rutkowski, A.-F., & Saunders, C. S. (2010). Growing pains with information overload. *Computer*, *43*(6), 94–95.

Acknowledgments

1. For a full review of the ideas of sociotechnical systems, see E. L. Trist and H. Murray (Eds.), *The social engagement of social science: A Tavistock anthology: The socio-technical perspective*, vol. II (Philadelphia: University of Pennsylvania Press, 1993).
2. Retrieved on 7/15/11 from http://TerriGriffith.com/blog
3. Retrieved on 7/15/11 from http://newwow.net/
4. Just one example: DeSanctis, G., & Poole, M. S. (1994). Capturing the complexity in advanced technology use: Adaptive structuration theory. *Organization Science*, *5*(2), 121–147.

ACKNOWLEDGMENTS

have been intrigued by the social and technical aspects of organizations and work for more than twenty years. In the world of academics we call this area "sociotechnical systems" and think about how organizations can be designed to jointly optimize the human and the technical.[1] Yet when was the last time you heard a manager talk about using sociotechnical ideas to design a change? I've been driven to find a way to make these important ideas more palatable outside the halls of universities. *The Plugged-In Manager* is the result, and I have many institutions, colleagues, friends, and family to thank for their help.

My students and blog readers have to come first. I teach organizational design and technology and innovation management to Silicon Valley professionals who are getting their MBAs while still doing their day jobs. This is a tough audience. Every day they see what happens when you aren't plugged in and wonder how to improve their own organizations. Frankly, this book is written to their bosses. My hope is that the ideas will provide an opening for my students to implement their new perspectives.

My students also get credit for my blog, Technology and Organizations.[2] How so? The students always ask excellent questions, but I was hearing many of the same questions every term.

The blog is a powerful knowledge management method in that I can give a single, thoughtful answer to a question rather than answer the same question across a range of quick emails. In giving me a reason to write the blog, my students also gave me a path to this book. Blogging is a great way to sneak up on a book. I've been able to test different ways of presenting the ideas, met interesting people (some of whom you've now read about), and benefited from readers' comments along the way. To them, many thanks for those comments—and please keep them coming.

Blogging is a start, but it is a long way to the finished product. There have been three versions of this project, and I am very thankful to those who helped with the evolution. Hoa Quach has been my research assistant, contact with the thinking of Gen Y, and sometime taskmaster. She stayed up late making editing passes and pestered her friends for their thoughts (she also introduced me to the joys of fancy food trucks). Seth Tator had this tough job at the earliest stages, and I hope he will enjoy the result.

The team at Jossey-Bass is incredibly supportive. (Thank you to Don Lamm, literary agent, and Andrew Hargadon, author of *How Breakthroughs Happen*, for the introductions.) Genoveva Llosa, my editor at Jossey-Bass, has been the project champion and inspiration for the final, and much improved, direction. I thank her for helping me to find the right niche and for seeing the possibilities at the early stages. Leslie Stephen has come to know each and every word in this book as she helped me move the style from professor to professional. She knew she was taking on a big task and has been a wonderful teacher along the way. I'm fortunate that Byron Schneider, also of Jossey-Bass, introduced me to Leslie, kept watch over the project during the revisions, and kept all the plates in the air. Thank you all, and I accept responsibility for any remaining errors.

The research behind *The Plugged-In Manager* is a longtime collaboration. Santa Clara University and the Leavey School of Business provided multiple grants in support of my research assistants, travel to collect data, and the time to focus on the topic. Thank you to the grant committees and the alumni who provided the resources.

Jay Brand, Brian Scott, and their company, Haworth, Inc., provided another kind of resource—their time, their thoughts, and access to their colleagues. They have written letters to grant committees, taken conference calls, and arranged for focus groups. I met Jay and Brian through the New Ways of Working Network, and I look forward to sharing this final result with the full group.[3]

Although my academic coauthors—John E. Sawyer, M. Scott Poole, and Robert E. McGrath—don't have their names on the cover of this book, what is behind the cover is a collaboration of years. John, Scott, Robert, and I work together on the research and publication of these ideas in peer-reviewed forums. These scholars have also been collaborators through their separate writing. This is especially true of Scott's work with Gerardine (Gerry) DeSanctis.[4] Thank you for letting me step away for these months to try spreading the word another way.

Nilofer Merchant and Ted Cocheu have been mentors as I learn to present these ideas to a broader audience. Nilofer is an alumna of Santa Clara University's MBA program, founder and CEO of Rubicon Consulting, author of *The New How*, and a member of the Leavey School of Business advisory board. Her ideas are highlighted in Chapters Two and Five, and her influence is also felt as she has modeled how one graciously, but forcefully, presents ideas. Ted Cocheu, founder and CEO of Altus, was one of my first contacts when I moved to Silicon Valley. It has been good Belgian beer and clam chowder as we sorted through what is and isn't important. He was especially helpful with the challenges of describing mixing, even to the point of writing test paragraphs.

Many others have helped to push these ideas through their various stages. Here I list just a subset of all the people who have been critics, confidants, and colleagues. Thank you to Dave Alpert, Hammel, Green and Abrahamson, Inc., for comments in the earliest stages and for organizing Expotition, a wonderful group of professionals interested in the infrastructure of work; David Armstrong, Santa Clara University, for hallway conversations that often ended with a 180-pound Newfoundland lying on my feet; Yekaterina Bezrukova, for camaraderie and access to her department's students; Emily Chung, Cisco, for always having interesting questions; Lynne Cooper, NASA's Jet Propulsion Lab, for feedback along the way; Gloria Hofer, Santa Clara University, for helping me find unique ways to present complex material; Tatyana Kanzaveli, Center for the Edge at Deloitte & Touche, for many introductions through her MeetUps and TEDx activities; Queene Mavor, Cisco, for letting me check my ideas against the real world; Margaret Neale, Stanford University, for being a role model and mentor; Gregory Northcraft, University of Illinois, for teaching me to write when inspired; Bob Waldron, for helping me to see how plugged-in management works in the world of electric aircraft; and Patrick Yam, Sensei Partners, for teaching me the ways of Silicon Valley, including the need for the occasional tennis and dim sum break.

I am grateful to all the plugged-in people who granted interviews and referred me to their own plugged-in colleagues. Whether your story is here or not, you are the foundation of this book: Col. Nate Allen, U.S. Army; Dr. James Brevig, Providence Regional Medical Center; Coco Brown, Taos Consulting; Michael Chui, McKinsey; Brett Colbert, NetApp; Mary Correia, Santa Clara University; Jay Cross, Internet Time; Stuart DeSpain, Microsoft; Judy Espedal, Providence Regional Medical Center; Evernote; Megan Gailey, Maxim Integrated Products; Keith Glynn, Zappos; Gunjan Gupta, Santa Clara University; David Hanson; Doyle Hopper, Nucor/Vulcraft; Jennifer Kenny, BizTH!NK; Ben Kepes, Diversity Analysis; Suzanne Kirkpatrick; Dan Krug, Nucor; Earl Lawrence, EAA; Eugene Lee, Socialtext; Susan Lucas-Conwell,

SDForum; Stuart Mader, CFA Institute; Ross Mayfield, Socialtext; Tad Milbourn, Intuit; Dirk Petersen, Nucor; Matt Pope, Microsoft; Barry Posner, Santa Clara University; Scott Schnaars, Badgeville; Dan Schultz, ASTM; Amelia Smith and the "Ask Anything" team, Zappos Insights; Kara Sprague, McKinsey; Eilif Trondsen, Strategic Business Insights; Kim Williams, Providence Regional Medical Center; Rhonda Winter, Indianapolis Motor Speedway; Jon Wolske, Zappos Insights; and Raymond Zammuto, University of Queensland.

I've mentioned that the inspiration and interest in these topics started long ago. I have two faculty members to thank for that. Professor Zur Shapira put the wheels in motion. He took me on as an unknown undergraduate research assistant, knew exactly the career advice to give me when I graduated, then made it possible for me to take that advice. He has been a friend and colleague all these years.

Zur advised me to work with Professor Paul S. Goodman at Carnegie-Mellon University. Paul taught me how to talk with people about their work. Our first interviews together were formal ones related to technology implementation in an auto assembly plant, but I recall a trip to the airport when I realized Paul would interview anyone, anywhere, about how and why they do their work the way they do. The SuperShuttle driver got to explain exactly how dispatching worked and the role that the console on his dash played. Paul has gone on to make PBS documentaries, including *The Dabbawallas*, describing how these people use no modern technologies and yet deliver lunch to over a hundred thousand workers in India with Six Sigma reliability.

Friends and family are behind any effort of consequence. Daryl Nish has kept my boat afloat while I have been an absentee skipper. Captain Emile Carles and the crew of Lelo Too managed to get me on the water for races and didn't complain when I was out of practice. Lynne Orloff-Jones has fed me more times than I can count. Luckily for me she's the author of several cookbooks.

My parents, Kay and Neil Griffith, gave me my love of reading, science, and technology. Michael and Renee Griffith are my technical and design consultants and the parents of my lovely nieces— what an amazing generation theirs will be! Bruce Whetstone joins me in my curiosity and passion for flight, space, and love.

ABOUT THE AUTHOR

Terri L. Griffith is a professor of management in the Leavey School of Business at Santa Clara University, California (Silicon Valley). Her office has an open door to graduate and undergraduate entrepreneurs who are trying to build plugged-in products, services, and organizations. Her award-winning blog, Technology and Organizations, is often inspired by the challenges her working students face.

Her research and consulting interests include the implementation and effective use of new technologies and organizational practices. This work most recently focuses on team tools and methods for innovation, though she has specialized in virtual/distributed collaboration since 1984. Terri's recent field research involves two Fortune 100 tech companies (funded by the National Science Foundation), both focused on generating the greatest value from their teams in complex environments. She has published over fifty articles, chapters, and reviews, as well as numerous academic presentations at national and global conferences. She was coeditor of the Technology volume of *Research on Managing Groups and Teams* (JAI Press, 2000).

Terri is also a sought-after research consultant to companies and associations. She has authored or coauthored reports for the Society for Information Management's Advanced Practices

Council, Cisco, and the New Ways of Working Network. Her recent speaking engagements and panel appearances include Yahoo! and EMC. She also has supervised student capstone projects for Google and NASA.

Terri began her studies in engineering at the University of California, Berkeley, but graduated with a bachelor of arts degree after becoming more interested in how technology is used than built. Her master's and doctoral degrees are from the Graduate School of Industrial Administration (now the Tepper School of Business) at Carnegie Mellon University. Both degrees were in organizational psychology and theory with a minor in technology.

Before coming to Santa Clara University, Terri was on the faculties of Washington University, St. Louis, and the University of Arizona. She has also held visiting positions at the University of California, Berkeley; Purdue University; Northwestern University; the Melbourne School of Business; and the Sasin Graduate Institute of Business Administration in Bangkok, Thailand. Her other international experience includes a United States Information Agency–funded "train the trainer" program in Bulgaria where she and other faculty presented U.S. business education topics and techniques.

She is a member of the Academy of Management, the Institute for Operations Research and the Management Sciences (INFORMS), and the Association for Information Systems. She is an editorial board member of *IEEE Transactions on Engineering Management*, the *Journal of Engineering and Technology Management*, and the *Journal of Managerial Issues*; a past senior editor for *Organization Science*; as well as a past associate editor for *MIS Quarterly*. Terri has coedited two journal issues focused on the academic issues underlying plugged-in management. For several years she was the convenor of the Organization Science Winter Conference, an annual think-tank event that draws academics as well as senior executives for discussions of cutting-edge research and practice.

INDEX

Mixing (continued)
138–139; assessing whether or
not to use wiki as example of,
74–79, 82–83, 178n4; BUILDER
checklist for designing, 79–84;
business transformation
consultant's views on, 115–116;
companies successfully using,
34–39, 84–85, 87–88; defined, 4,
33, 63–64; example of
consequences of not using,
85–87; example of organization
practicing, 162–163; moving
expenses with new job as
example of, 71–73; negotiation
steps as framework for, 65–73; as
plugged-in practice, 8; value of,
64–65, 170; wiki as tool for, 64;
wiki use by new CEO as example
of, 68–70, 71, 72
Moving expenses, negotiating,
71–73

N

NASA Innovation Incubator, 50
Need-to-share, shift from need-to-
know to, 23–25
Negotiation: issue-by-issue, 78,
179n7; of moving expenses with
new job, 71–73; steps in, as
framework for Mixing, 65–73
The New How (Merchant), 25–26,
105–106
1984 (Orwell), 140–142
Nucor: culture of, 142–144;
on-the-job learning by new hires
at, 95–97; response to flooding,
144–146
Nucor Steel, 146–149

O

Observation, 8, 45–46
Ochman, B. L., 52–53
O'Connor, Edward, 44
Open Leadership (Li), 17
Openness. *See* Transparency

Organizational processes, as
building blocks of organizations,
3, 6
Organizations: building blocks of, 3,
6; complexity of, 11, 12, 16–19;
example of plugged-in
management practiced by,
160–166; plugging in necessary
for success of, 3–5
O'Toole, James, 25, 32

P

Palfrey, John, 20–21
PARC, 47; Living Laboratory, 50
Pasteur, Louis, 61
People: as building blocks of
organizations, 3, 6; diversity of,
13, 19–21; highlighting,
practicing plugged-in
management, 100–102;
importance of, when
implementing change, 114–117;
interdependence of, 93; tips on
introducing technology to,
97–100
Petersen, Dirk, 144, 146–148
Plain Talk (Iverson), 143–144
Plugged-in management: avoiding
jargon when introducing, 92–95;
business transformation
consultant's insights on applying,
114–117; case study of, 34–39;
current need for, 3–5, 11;
example of layered method of
practicing, 160–166;
organizational conditions
creating need for, 13–21; public
practice of, 105–108; required
throughout organization, 6–7;
systemic changes creating need
for, 21–30
Plugged-in practices, 7–9, 33–34. *See
also* Mixing; Sharing;
Stop-Look-Listen
Plugging-in skill: defined, 2;
importance of, 7, 169–171; value